Notes From a Practicing Writer

The Craft, Career, and Aesthetic of Playwriting

Volume One

ED SHOCKLEY'S
REPRESENTATION:

Shockley Foundation
2100 Chestnut Street
2nd floor
Philadelphia, PA 19103

Also visit:

www.EdShockley.com

www.YouthPlays.com

Notes from a Practicing Writer

The Craft, Career, and Aesthetic of Playwriting

Volume One

by Ed Shockley
edited by Lary Moten

Hopewell Publications

NOTES FROM A PRACTICING WRITER: Volume One
Copyright © 2007 by Ed Shockley

Published by
Hopewell Publications, LLC
PO Box 11, Titusville, NJ
08560-0011 (609) 818-1049

info@HopePubs.com
www.HopePubs.com

Library of Congress Cataloging of Publishing Data
Shockley, Ed.-
  Notes from a practicing writer / Ed Shockley.
    p. cm.
  Includes bibliographical references.
  ISBN 0-9726906-3-8 (v. 1 : alk. paper)
  1. Playwriting. I. Title.
  PN1661.S56 2005
  808.2—dc22

                                                      2005003031

Second Edition

Printed in the United States of America

If a single phrase inspires,
then this effort is worth my life.

TABLE OF CONTENTS

ACKNOWLEDGEMENTS

In a long career there are so many people to thank that any attempt will inevitably ignore and offend moreso than praise and exault. I acknowledge here by name the individuals who were recruited specifically for the creation of this book, author Christopher Klim, Lary Moten, Sara Savitz, and Bill Rolleri. I give thanks for the sacrifices and support of my sons, wife, mother, grandmother and two fathers. The innumerable artists, mentors and educators who have collaborated in more than a quarter century of theatrical explorations have all either been mentioned in the essays that comprise this book or their ideas shamelessly stolen and repeated as if they were my original thoughts.

I humbly offer this collection of observations to all the students of art who labor alone in the belief that "the right word, in the right ear, at the right time, will change the world."

PREFACE

Every time that I pick up my pen I am overwhelmed with dichotomous emotions. First there is a grandiose sense of elation as I consider the possibilities suggested by the blank page that I will soon fill with brilliant ramblings. Next, the infinite possibilities for choice that precede every word and phrase, every choice of plot and character, every aspect of drama, all combine to stagger me. Finally the impossibility of my creation ever equaling the perfect vision that was its inspiration almost overwhelms me.

South African novelist Ezekiel Mpelele says that he is a "practicing writer." This is the perfect term to describe the chaos that is my artistic process. I bumble through a manuscript much like a vegetable vendor's carthorse. In place of a carrot I pursue the cathartic words "the end" across line after line and page after page of scrawl.

Oscar Wilde is credited with the adage, "Plays aren't written they're re-written." That over quoted bit of wit has proven my salvation. If only I can fill enough pages then I trust that trial and error, edit and revision, will inevitably transform my mountain of words into a taunt and compelling drama.

At the start of my career I posted letters to any author whose address I could finagle. I asked only one question…

"How do you begin a play?"

The most practicable response that I received was from Richard Wesley, author of *The Mighty Gents*. He replied simply…

"I start writing."

Every semi-literate who fills a page is guilty of being a writer. Most are bad writers but that should not intimidate anyone. Have you ever read those early short plays by Eugene O'Neill? Are you aware that Henrik Ibsen wrote *The Warrior's Barrow* long before he explored *A Doll's House*? One could argue that these novice tomes suggest future greatness but it does not take the imagination of a Pirandello to picture how pathetic their first drafts must have been.

Luckily, greatness is assigned according to the merits of the final draft of one's best play. A. Marcus Hemphill wrote twenty-two versions of *Inacent Black* before it reached Broadway and bombed. I suppose that statistic should not frighten a sincere writer. Anyone who wrestles with words because they must, because a demanding dybbuk torments them, that someone will be inspired by the inexorability of Marcus' march to the Great White Way. His example demonstrates that one need only relentlessly pursue the best in oneself, page by page, and success is assured. (*Inacent Black* eventually ran two years off-Broadway and Marcus went on to write for the historic *Cosby Show*.)

If I were pressed to voice some specific and succinct suggestion to offer compatriot practicing writers then it would be four words...

"Write. Analyze. Write again."

e. shockley

SECTION ONE

THE CRAFT OF PLAYWRITING

*"You can make most things harder
with a little effort."*
journal entry 4/12/98

*"Take the best from the better
and the better from the worst."
journal entry 12/23/78*

WRITING FOR ACTORS

Due to the difficulties of producing a short play festival, I once ended up on-stage performing two extended monologues that had to be hastily memorized. The experience made me cognizant of what actors require as they interpret our written works.

CHARACTER INFORMATION

Actors strive to lose themselves in the character. This is achieved by considering the information supplied by the author or implied by the text and situation. The character description that precedes a play is extremely helpful *if* the choices are not arbitrary and actually impact upon the play—Richard III's hump[1] and club

---

[1] see *Richard the Third* by William Shakespeare.

foot, Helen's[2] sensuality, or Walter Lee's[3] chauffeur job for instance.

The most exciting discoveries are those that are gleaned from scene study that can then be applied to give flesh to a character. Consider the following: "...(T)he key changes but the theme's the same," spoken by Danton in Georg Buchner's *Danton's Death*.[4] This declaration causes one to think of a character as being either a musician or an appreciator of music. The former choice affects the length of one's fingernails, for example. The latter choice sends the actor to a music library searching out the composer whose work expresses the soul of the character.

CHARACTER ACTION

Most American actors have read *Respect For Acting* by Uta Hagen. Her adage "Acting is doing," has been a mantra for at least two generations of performers. Words in a text take meaning from the actions that inform them and at the same time inspire action. Imagine, for example, two characters arguing in the early morning in pajamas. When one says, "Get your breath out of my face," a physicality is implied. Transpose the same argument to a bar at two a.m. and the words are redefined. A rich, germane, physical life inspires an actor.

---

[2] see *Trojan Women* by Aeschylus, *Helen* by Euripides.

[3] see *A Raisin in the Sun* by Lorraine Hansberry.

[4] see *Danton's Death* by Georg Buchner

LANGUAGE/DIALOGUE

Actors study text like monks study scripture. They operate in the belief that all of the answers are hidden there. This intense attention invests words with enormous meaning. This is especially true for repeated words — Al Pacino's "Hu-Hah" in *Scent of a Woman*. One of the worst crimes of authorship is to repeat words without intention and thus send actors off on a frenzied chase leading nowhere. What is worse is repetition that does not advance the play by redefining meaning so that the words function like booby-traps in the memorization process.

The second most common complaint among actors is the pretty line that's peanut butter in your mouth — "I ate eight oranges!" spoken at argument pitch. The plays of Seneca are mummified to this day because of his disregard for the theatrical reality.

> *"They say the mastiff Cerebus has broken loose and haunts the living. Earth herself's been heard to howl; hypertrophied phantoms stalk our woodlands, where the trembling trees shake down snow from their branches."*
>
> Oedipus *by Seneca, Act I Scene I*

THE MAGIC "WHAT IF?"

Acting guru Konstantin Stanislavski instructed actors in the Moscow Arts Theatre to recurrently ask the question, "What if?" The practice reveals a web of connected possibilities bordered by the realities of the text. "What if" Ma Rainey[5] is bisexual and is as jealous of the trumpet player as she is of her strumpet?" The director's task is to illuminate the themes of the play, but the actor's job is to convey the reality of the character leading us toward those themes.

American playwright Sydney Howard penned *They Knew What They Wanted*. In this play a lonely old farmer uses the picture of a young ranch hand to conscript a mail order bride. The play ends with the hireling leaving and the young lady reconciling herself to honoring the contract with her aged fiancé.

Eugene O'Neill read this play and asked, "What if" the ranch hand was written as the son of a hard as nails old farmer? Suddenly the inheritance of the farm is at issue. The woman falls in lustful love with the sullen young twerp and murders their baby to prove that she wasn't scheming to get the land. These alterations produced the American classic *Desire Under the Elms.*

The writer's challenge is to create a consistent world that inspires his/her collaborators to discover the truth or questions of life.

***

---

[5] see *Ma Rainey's Black Bottom*, by August Wilson.

"Traveling in inches a distance of miles..."
journal entry 1/28/86

"WHAT DOES A _____ DO?"

The title refers to an improvisational game I first witnessed during an audition at Theatre for a New Audience in New York. In the traditional application a group of actors sit in a circle. Each is instructed that he/she must rise and perform one physical action that defines the chosen character for the round. The aim of the game is to exhaust all rational possibilities.

In this example, "What does a writer do?"

Actor #1 mimes typing
Actor #2 writes with a pen
Actor #3 reads a book
Actor #4 paces the floor

Actor #5 smokes a cigarette
Actor #6 drinks.
Actor #7 chokes on an aspirin
  bottle cap.

The first time through, the choices tend to be focused largely on a single aspect of the character's life. When the exercise continues and the obvious choices are exhausted, then the focus broadens beyond the character as occupation and acknowledges the character as person. Writers talk on the telephone or cell phone, eat in restaurants, mow the lawn, massage tired wrists, etc.

What the exercise teaches writers is that there are actions that define specific characters and a little digging unearths more novel attributes.

Applying this tool to the literary process involves playing the game in your head or, better still, in your journal. The goal is to find the choice that is "most dramatically revealing."

1. He shoots a rifle.
2. He pours in powder.
3. He tamps it down with a rod.
4. He bayonets.
5. He fires a pistol.
6. He dies.
7. He writhes in pain.
8. He punches.
9. He waves a sword.
10. He hides.
11. He runs.
12. He coughs from powder smoke.
13. He lights the fuse on a cannon.
14. He digs graves.
15. He searches for body parts.
16. He writes letters to survivors.
17. He consoles widows.
18. He wipes up blood.
19. He carries the wounded.
20. He raises a flag.

Mountain[6] is my play about the decisive battle in the southern campaign of the War for American Independence. "What does a Patriot soldier do?"

The list could continue for pages. The question becomes, again, which image is most dramatic? What best reveals the nature of the character you are writing and the context of the moment?

---

[6] *Mountain* is an unpublished play in verse by Ed Shockley commissioned by the Children's Theatre of Charlotte.

Mountain opens with a battle that does not include the central figures of the play. Instead it presents an event that inspires them to seek revenge, the driving action of the drama. My solution is to begin with a character, the Unknown Soldier, decrying the madness of war amidst a mass of corpses reenacting their deaths at the Waxaw massacre. The audience then learns where they are, what has happened, why the survivors are incensed, etc. They also are prepared to anticipate the gory battle that ends the play but will resonate with more emotional force. Why? Because the characters dying will no longer be anonymous.

Ultimately this is a tool intended to inspire surprising stage pictures and character depth. Does a plumber constantly clean his fingernails? Does an athlete pick at acne that results from steroid use? A writer must perpetually ask...

> ***How can I more specifically
> define character and context?***

***

"Even when I whisper
there's a wish to be heard."
journal entry 3/21/94

OBJECTIVES AND TACTICS

Directors and actors are usually thinking in different terms than authors. There are no "lines" in a play, there are "moments." A character has a personality that is revealed through her/his choice of tactics in pursuit of objectives.

CHARACTERS PURSUE OBJECTIVES RELENTLESSLY

They employ a succession of tactics in pursuit of these objectives. The tactics used reveal personality and advance our plays. Contained therein is one of the simplest formulas for dynamic dramatic writing and an unerring tool for play revision.

During a rehearsal in North Carolina[7], for example, director Scott Miller asked that I consider changing a line,

---

[7] This exchange occurred during revisions rehearsals for the third remounting of *Nobody's Listening* by Ed Shockley

"...make this show mean something." He wanted the character to say, "...be real." Always in such instances I take the suggestions home and sleep on them, then deliver the revised pages for morning rehearsals.

Many times directors and actors think in different terms than authors. There are no "lines" in a play, there are "moments." A character has a personality that is revealed through her/his choice of tactics in pursuit of objectives.

The moment in question: a young man, Louis, is explaining to adults why he sabotaged a live television broadcast. His objective is to speak through the show both "to" and "for" the youth of America. His father had been murdered in an act of senseless violence, and this is an opportunity to redress that wrong. His tactic is to create emotional truth by provoking an actor into shooting him contrary to the script guidelines. It doesn't matter to Louis if the show is "real." In fact, the broadcast —about a mechanical boy in a public high school— could never be taken as anything other than fantasy. Instead he is committed to any course of action that causes the program to have a legitimate impact on the lives of viewers.

Armed with an accurate analysis of the character's aims, the writer can then complete a successful revision of dialogue. The actual issue for director and actor is the fact that Louis does not express his contempt for the program that he destroys. The final revision therefore becomes, "...make this *silly* show mean something."

WHY IS SOMETHING AS SMALL AS A WORD WORTH SUCH ATTENTION?

The words of our moments lead artists to discover the author's intentions. The tactics of a character, when arranged in escalating intensity, convey an audience inexorably to the climax and theme of our writing. To paraphrase an old Yiddish adage...

*"Take care of the objectives
and the play will take care of itself."*

***

*"Without a sense of truth
then the writing is nothing"
journal entry 1/5/86*

CREATING EMOTIONAL FULLNESS

Emotional fullness is a phrase popularized by Sanford Meisner[8] as a description of one of the primary goals of an actor. It is best described as a state of emotional arousal that exists prior to one's entrance into a scene.

Meisner's classic example is an actor who daily would attempt to pull the fire escape loose from its moorings in the wall before entering to confront a character on-stage.

The premise in this approach is that the arousing event need not lead literally into the emotions of the character but must be rooted in a "real" activity. This represents a distinct break from the practice of "sense memory" which Meisner eschews. Using the memory of a past experience, according to Meisner, threatens to place an actor outside of the stage reality.

---

[8] see *On Being an Actor* by Sanford Meisner for a more in depth analysis of emotional fullness.

This debate between the disciples of Stanislavski is relevant to writers only inasmuch as it demonstrates the impact of the prior life of a character on performance and emotional tone. In other words, Mary coming from a pleasant dinner is a different person than Mary getting off a New York rush hour subway train that has stalled.

An analysis points to simple and effective questions during the process of revision.

1. *Where is each character coming from prior to this entrance?*
2. *Is this the place that makes him most emotionally full?*
3. *What has happened in that place?*
4. *Does this make him most emotionally full?*
5. *What did he expect to encounter when he entered?*
6. *Does this make him most emotionally full?*
[Are you noticing a pattern?]

By supplying the actor with a concrete set of explosive circumstances, the choices of all the characters can be integrated into a far more incendiary dramatic web. Bob entering from changing the hoses on his truck reverberates through the scene and inspires perhaps white doilies on the end tables, gifts from a mother-in-law who sat next to a coughing man on the bus from Pittsburgh. Perhaps it's flu season. Of course the truck never got started.

"The choices made control the tone of our scenes."

***

"If it's not one thing, then it's something."
journal entry 6/27/92

THE BARKING DOG

An anonymous student writer at Lower Merion High School happened upon this tool. During a performance of his labored play, a neighborhood dog periodically barked to the delight of the otherwise dissatisfied audience. It was due in part to the fervor of the actress rendering the vocalization. It was also successful because of the element of surprise. What is most important is that it worked. Recognizing successful tools is what makes successful writers.

Analyzing the phenomenon enabled us to postulate guidelines to govern the use of this device.

- *The sound must be germane to the world of the play.*
- *It is best used to break the monotony of a long passage.*

- *It is a less consequential device than "symbolic ambient sound," as in the baying hounds during the final scene of Langston Hughes' antebellum drama* Mulatto[9].
- *The tendency toward a comic response increases with each usage.*

Basically an author need only identify a working conflict with an overlong trajectory (i.e. "The scene is just too slow."). List one dozen sounds and/or events from the world of your play. (Barking dogs, boiling teapots, chapel bells). Insert the most relevant or "germane" into the text to inspire a release of energy, relieving the doldrums long enough to reach your climactic moment with the audience in tow.

Try it and see. Remember *Citizen Kane's* cockatoo? No great symbolic icon, just a plain old-fashioned natural noise to give the audience a gentle jolt and cause them to listen more closely for a few moments.

They won't get it
if they aren't encouraged to pay attention.

***

---

[9] *Mulatto* by Langston Hughes was the first Black play to appear on Broadway and ends when the illegitimate son of a plantation owner is killed by his mother rather than allowing him to suffer the torture of an approaching lynch mob.

"Dialogue is action."
journal entry 9/28/92

COMPRESSION

Compression is a straightforward tool of revision that involves replacing undemonstrative words with character specific information. The goal is to "compress" more details into the same verbal space.

Let's begin with three statements made by a character that we will call...

```
              JOE
    She was a pretty girl. No, a
beautiful girl. The most beautiful
girl I've seen in a long time.
```

What do we learn about this man? Joe thinks this girl is very attractive. He likes girls. He qualifies his thoughts. She is either physically striking or he hasn't been around women much lately.

These same three ideas after a compression revision can inspire a much richer picture of character on several levels.

```
          JOE                          JESUS
She  was  a  pretty         She  was  a  hammer,
girl.  No,  a               bro.  A  ballpene  hammer
beautiful  girl.            with  skin  as  smooth
The  most  beautiful        as  fresh-sanded  pine-
girl  linda  I've           wood.  I  ain't  seen
seen  in  a  long           such  a  muchacha  since
time.                       I  left  San  Juan.
```

A comparison of the two monologues illuminates the process and product of compression. We learn that Jesus is an immigrant from San Juan, Puerto Rico. We know that he learned English in east coast urban America. He is either a carpenter or uses wood in some hobby activity. He has met a woman who has made him homesick. She is probably young ("smooth skin," "muchacha").

An actor and audience can more easily hitch their wagons to a compressed character. The cumbersome exposition that playwright Bruce Graham describes as "sugar coated throat rams" is circumnavigated by dispatching it during dramatic action.

```
                    MERCER
          I don't like cops.

                    DANON
          Is that right?

                    MERCER
          It's a black thing.

                    DANON
          Well, I don't like cons; it's a
     cop thing. 10
```

This exchange demonstrates that information about one character can be compressed into the dialogue of another. Mercer in this beat reveals an attitude toward authority. Danon in turn delivers emotional and factual revelations. Both statements resonate in the minds of the audience and incite a process of questioning.

We wonder what experiences have shaped Mercer's perspective. We wonder if there will be some consequence for his outspokenness. Danon identifies Mercer as an ex-con and communicates an inherent enmity. We anticipate unfair, or at least indelicate, subsequent interactions.

Every character speaks in a unique patois that reveals the specifics of their personality and ethnography. This subliminal information positions the audience to effec-

---

[10] excerpt from *A Salt Water Oasis* by e. shockley.

tively interpret the stage behavior and thereby encounter the themes of the play.

Once begun, an author can go insane with compression. Each character can use metaphors from their profession or homeland. The couch potato may sample television jingles, the jockey can measure a bureau in "hands."

Ultimately this device requires that we look more closely at the details of our characters' lives and make specific choices. Only good things can come of such an effort.

The simple fact is that a finite number of plots have been revisited continually since the start of human history —loss, betrayal, love, discovery, salvation, damnation... the human condition. The inherent sameness of our writing suggests that style is more important than subject in deciding the acceptance of a play.

Imagine if each occupant of your imaginary world revealed subtle sociological information with every utterance. Consider the thrill of discovery for both actor and audience when class, vocation, age, culture, era, religion, et al., are carefully constructed and skillfully introduced simultaneously with unfolding dramatic action. This is what separates Shakespeare's Juliet from a Susan Lucci made-for-TV movie.

> *Specificity is the foundation*
> *upon which universality is achieved.*

***

*"It unnerves me to remember
that yesterday today was tomorrow."
journal entry 1/30/92*

PROJECTION

Clay Goss[11] introduced this exercise to me during a Temple University graduate conference. It has proven helpful when a work stalls because of "undynamic characters."

Firstly, choose a character from your play and project that person into the future twenty years. The ultimate goal of this exercise is to create interesting people, so it is wise to transport forward to some moment either of great success or tragedy.

Secondly, define clearly the physical and cultural reality of the character in this new environment. Is the person now an alcoholic, suicidal, president, celibate, etc.)

Next, return to the present and incorporate the seeds of this future self into the current situation. The key

---

[11] Author of *Home Cooking: Five Plays;* and co-author with Linda Goss of *Jump Up and Say: A Collection of Black Storytelling,* Touchstone Press.

is making conscious to the audience the implied future of your character.

For example, Joe is afraid of losing his job so he won't speak out about racial insensitivity at Texaco. Projecting him forward reveals he is a business manager for a corporation laundering drug monies through a fuel oil front in Mexico. He has ulcers and has replaced his loving wife with a mindless waif who likes to spend money more than time with him.

Returning to the present I make Joe someone who rifles through waste paper baskets looking for information on co-workers. His real name is Jose, but he denies his Mexican father. He got through college paying engineering students to take his lecture hall tests and has married a classmate because her pedigree gives him access into high society. Of course, he is having an affair with his blonde secretary.

Fill each character with a richly textured back-story that thrills actors and moves audiences.

***

*"Playwriting is like an old puzzle.
You don't know if all of the pieces are there
or if they will fit until it is done."
journal entry 2/19/79*

REDUCTION[12]

Recently, I was forced to teach prose writing to a group of middle school students on an Amish farm near Intercourse, Pennsylvania. I say "forced" because playwriting is my area of expertise; and while I might squeeze out an occasional story or essay, I haven't a notion as to how to instruct someone else to do it.

The weekend was not a total disaster. I grew accustomed to the aggressive smells that accompany farm living and managed to communicate my love of writing to the assembled youth. In fact, through no fault of mine, we even managed to generate a dozen essays, monologues and one overly long play.

More importantly, at least within the context of this book, is an exercise peculiar to story writing that has direct applications in the process of playsmithing. In this

---

[12] Originally printed in the now defunct *Philly Beat Magazine*.

drill I had my wards tell a story in five simple sentences. Adjectives and adverbs were outlawed. Participles were accepted grudgingly. The idea was to tell your tale in fifteen key words.

Let's take a story that we all know: *A Raisin in the Sun.*

This sprawling narrative might be reduced to:

1. *Mother inherits money.*
2. *Mother finds house.*
3. *Son finds business.*
4. *Son squanders money.*
5. *Family buys house.*

In my retelling of it, Ms. Hansberry's classic melodrama is a play about a family finding a new balance after the death of its patriarch. Clybourne Park (the all-white neighborhood where Mama decides on a new house) and the racial conflict are exposed to be of diminished importance. This sub-theme makes the play more socially relevant for the audience of its time but could be omitted without altering the central theme.

Notes, however, is an examination of the tools of playcraft not dramaturgy; so let's abandon Lorraine and focus instead upon this marvelous little fifteen-word device for discerning the essential in a narrative.

The most practical applications occur when we are stuck. The process of reduction gives us something to do until the Muses return. There is never a time when we cannot write three words.

It is possible, additionally, to clarify a plot by restating one or more of our reduced sentences. Suppose, for example, that I began a reduction of Tennessee Williams' *A Streetcar Named Desire* with:

>   1. *Blanche visits Stella.*
>   2. *Stanley is suspicious.*

I might rework my concept as;

>   1. *Stanley is happy.*
>   2. *Blanche attacks Stanley.*

Both reductions might inspire a first scene between the two sisters but the latter volunteers a clue as to the content of the moment. "Happy" communicates more information than "visits." The scene now can be constructed to convey an anxious calm that quickly is shattered by Blanche's pretensions.

The reality of writing is that each blank page is an enemy. The limitless choices that it represents are near to overwhelming. Reduction is a device that serves to constrict the range of options confronting us. It is applicable to the entire play or within the context of a single scene. I just wish I had stumbled upon it ten years earlier. Perhaps there wouldn't be quite so much gray in my hair today.

Any practice that constricts the range of options is a welcome addition to your toolbox.

***

"Nothing's ever written by a pen that does not move." journal entry 1/22/85

THE ILLUSION OF WRITER'S BLOCK

HYSTERICAL BLINDNESS

If "the ability to see" is what makes us writers, then writer's block is akin to hysterical blindness. The cure is embodied in admitting: a) the psychosomatic quality of the condition, b) effective diagnosis of the literary process and then c) the application of specific finite tactics to advance a script.

Is there ever, for instance, a moment when an author cannot write a bad line? Obviously not. The block then is largely a result of critical thinking. Either there are too many possible choices or what has been considered is found to be unsatisfactory.

An important next question becomes, "Why don't I like this choice?" Once this is effectively answered using analytical rather than critical language, literary solutions become instantly evident. A more thorough analysis includes the question, "Why?" Criticism is an emotional response to writing. "It's not clever." "It sucks." "I can do better." All of those are critical, subjective, reactive responses. "The protagonist stopped making witty retorts" is a contrasting example of proactive analysis.

WONDER WHERE THE DRAMA WENT?

Another common dramatic problem that results in stalled projects is a dissipation of dramatic tension. The next line or action won't come because no one on-stage seems motivated to act. Two very simple tactics address this situation:

> 1. *Go back to the last moment wherein someone strongly wanted something. Find who or what opposes this desire and increase their efficacy.*
>
> ### *OR*
>
> 2. *Return to the construction of the characters and change their histories to increase both their natural antipathy and the dynamic quality of their needs.*

At Temple University and again at the New York Black Writers Conference, I conducted an informal experiment in perception. Several subjects stood at varying distances from a classroom wall with their eyes closed. They were asked to open them for a single second then close them again.

Each described what they had seen. The responses generally fell into two categories. Either the viewer remembered a single spot on the wall or a generalized picture of the area.

As writers we are informed by the phenomenon that there are two conceptual approaches to examining one's work. Often when a microcosmic analysis is unproductive, a shift to a macrocosmic perspective will re-energize our efforts or vice versa.

Specifically, focusing on story when dialogue stalls or introducing props when plot sputters can revitalize the writing. Theme is macrocosmic; action, microcosmic. Rarely do both become derailed simultaneously.

Once the characters of a play are clearly drawn, it is a practicable matter to ask them to act. By focusing upon what someone is doing rather than what they are saying, an author is inspired to introduce dynamic actions into the text, which will move the play dramatically forward. Is there ever a time when we cannot introduce an action into a scene?

YOU HAVE FOUR OTHER SENSES, YOU KNOW

Often in early drafts of texts I am amazed at how reliant I become on the single sense of sight. Remember that, philosophical arguments aside, we encounter the world through five senses that offer a useful set of tools to advance one's writing.

Bill and Betty are trapped in a cloakroom and the author is stuck for words. "What is that smell?" "It's my sandwich." "Is that you making that scratching noise?" "What are you doing?" "It's hot in here and the sweat makes these wool pants itch." "Is there any alcohol in this punch?"

Every arbitrary creative tool suggested here arises from a single premise. "In order to do things, you have to do things."[13] Any activity that moves a pen solves a problem. Once an author resumes writing then insightful analysis of what's written reveals either its appropriateness or an alternative.

Also, by arriving somehow at the next moment, one is able to see farther into the darkness and thereby consider more complete solutions to dramatic challenges.

YA HEAD HOITS... 'TIL YA BANG YER KNEE

Ernie Schier, former lead critic for the now defunct *Philadelphia Bulletin* daily newspaper, suggested the last and most certain solution to the illusion of writer's block. So many decades have passed that I can only paraphrase his idea, but in essence he advised that you could always start another play. Eventually that project will encounter some difficulty and, if you're lucky, it will make the problems of the first work seem surmountable by comparison.

When it all seems poised to overwhelm you, remember that were you to pen a single page per day you would be one of the most prolific authors in all of human history. What's that—a dozen lines and four stage directions?

Get on with it... then go have a chocolate frappe.

***

---

[13] Quote of Sidney from Lorraine Hansberry's *The Sign in Sidney Brustein's Window*.

SECTION TWO

THE ART OF PLAYWRITING

"The Science of Playwriting, that is what I'm practicing. Experiments in style, structure, genre, et al, in order to heal society"
journal entry 11/18/94

*"There are things one has to
learn anew every day"
journal entry 1/28/93*

WORDS TO WRITE BY

The ability to write well is defined entirely by one's facility to "see." Recognizing what is working and what needs work is the prescription for literary success. The following are quotes from dramatists and theorists that illuminate the theatrical process. By choosing a quote and analyzing a specific piece of your writing in light of it, the strengths and weaknesses of your voice will become clearer.

"The dramatist must picture life in action, with an unpreoccupied mind, as the musician pictures her in sound and the sculptor in form."

W.B. Yeats

"..theatre...an opportunity to experience imaginative life as physical presence."

David Cole

"A play is a world. The language of a play displays and defines the nature of that world."

David Rabe

"Farce and melodrama depend upon action that is unrelated to character."

Anonymous

"The drama's laws the drama's patrons give."

Ben Jonson

"Dialogue must appear to be spoken in context yet rise above it."

Anonymous

"...the most economical, the least time consuming, the most elegant expression of thought will be nearest to the truth.'

Occam's Razor

"I don't represent reality in a play, I present a reality to the spectator."

Durremat

"Freedom is not achieved by working freely."

Tennessee Williams

"Action is character."

F. Scott Fitzgerald

"A hero in a traditional drama was a person who willed something hard enough to act in order to achieve it."

Alan Reynolds Thompson

"A stage setting is not a background, it is an environment."
Anonymous

"[Comedy is] *the sudden transformation of a strained expectation into nothing."*
Kant

"It helps when obstacles can be personified."
Ed Shockley

"My only obligation is to survive and write."
James Baldwin

***

"Wisdom is the chief part of happiness."

Sophocles

DOES IT HAVE TO FLY?

One quiet Sunday afternoon, playwright and former TV headliner Tony Buck shared reminiscences of his employment at Rolls Royce. A key aspect of their philosophy was captured in the phrase, "Does it have to fly?"

The example he gave to illustrate this concept was a story of a worker sent to a scrap yard to fetch a ten-meter piece of metal. An exhausting search turned up nine- and eleven-meter rods but no piece of the required length was available among the remnants.

A supervisor arrived and interrupted the young man's frenzied efforts to shave a piece of tempered steel down to size. The older worker took the rod and proceeded to prop open the lid of a trash bin. "It doesn't need to fly."

There are times when painstaking precision is required and other moments when a metal wedge is enough. The trick is knowing which moment you are in.

During my tenure as assistant to literary manager Cynthia Jennings at American Place Theatre, I quickly learned to pass over unsolicited scripts bound in expensive leather covers. (Our instructions were to read all of the priority plays then the first eight pages of the others if time permitted.) Writers who invested that much wealth in a draft of an unproduced play either got the printing done for free or hadn't committed to the revision process.

What does this mean? Each of us must be brave. We must dedicate ourselves to the best plays within us and use all available facilities made to hone our craft rather than advance our careers or massage our egos. (The latter two events are natural byproducts of the successful completion of the first.)

Visiting an Intro Theatre class at Davidson College, I listened to the answers from undergraduates to the question, "Why go to the theatre?" After they completed the obligatory kissing up to the professor by offering whatever answer they imagined he wanted to hear, they unanimously conceded that they go to see their friends or fulfill assignments.

There are lines at concerts, summer cinema releases and sporting events but theatres consider 60% houses successful runs. I suggest that our projects "are not flying."

Often our efforts are intended to create competent works. "It's not that bad" is an all too frequent assessment of a developing work. Personally, I do not want the word "bad" spoken at all in conjunction with my work unless it is interpreted ebonically.

Writers stand in awe of Williams, Shakespeare and O'Neill as if those authors were endowed with divine gifts beyond the ken of mortals. I suggest that an examination of *Titus Andronicus, Hello From Bertha, The Dreamy Kid*, etc., reveals that the primary difference between historic authors and hacks is embodied in the Rolls Royce principal.

As we continue to encourage and respect one another, I ask that we also devote ourselves to nothing less than air-worthy vessels.

No qualifiers, excuses or rationalizations;
we <u>know</u> it has to fly.

***

"Intellect guides...but emotion rules."
journal entry 9/17/85

AUTHOR AS EGGHEAD

A short while ago I assisted in the search for a band to perform at a fundraiser for the now defunct Venture Theatre Company. The audience was an equal mix of adolescents and older adults.

The first band had never heard of "Misty." The next group was versant in 50's jazz and pop but their R & B repertoire ended when Eddie Kendricks[14] went solo.

We listened to the tape of a band that played all of the songs in the same key, one that played two speeds, slow and less slow, and my personal favorite, the group that knew every type of music but no one could read so they had to be provided with tapes of any new songs to be learned.

Each of these artists was at best under-qualified as a musician and possibly incompetent. A professional performer is expected to read lead sheets and scores, trans-

---

[14] Former lead singer for the Temptations.

pose, and demonstrate a passing acquaintance with the various musical styles.

Most of the better writers that I have been privileged to meet consistently discuss their creations in musical terminology. Words like rhythm, crescendo, staccato, symphony, motive, beats, etc. are constantly on the tongues of Charles Fuller,[15] Garland Lee Thompson,[16] Richard Wesley[17] and Marian X[18].

It seems that the abstract clarity of composition cuts through much of the confusion engendered by words. We are rarely, for example, equivocate in our assessment of a vocalist in the same way we are with actors or writers.

Imagine the great orchestra leader Duke Ellington's[19] response to a saxophonist who only played in a single key? What about a drummer who couldn't produce a Salsa foundation for a Dizzy Gillespie[20] tune? When we call ourselves "players" we are assumed to know all major, minor and altered scales, musical styles, sight reading, et al.

What are the equivalent skills for the playwright? How would those skills be identified? The standards, I suppose, are the texts and authors that define genres.

---

[15] Pulitzer prize winning author of *A Soldier's Play*.

[16] Co-founder and Artistic Director of Frank Silvera Writers' Workshop.

[17] Author of *The Mighty Gents*.

[18] 1997 PEW Fellowship winner. Author of *Wet Carpets*.

[19] Historic bandleader and composer.

[20] Jazz trumpeter considered one of the original fathers of "bebop."

Strindberg,[21] Aeschylus,[22] Moliere,[23] Shakespeare, Orton,[24] Baraka,[25] Ibsen,[26] Shange,[27] Churchill.[28] Facility means mastery of dialogue, plot, pacing, character building, and so forth.

One never finds musicians ridiculed for studying European classical music or worrying about "losing their voice." Yet authors routinely cite such an argument to justify anti-intellectualism. Imagine where Shakespeare or Sean "Diddy" Combs[29] would be without the ubiquitous "samplings" that inspired their greatest works?

Just as musicians scour popular folk and classical archives of various nations, so we authors must also immerse ourselves in the creations, styles and theatrical

---

[21] August Strindberg's *Miss Julie* is a classic model of naturalism and his *Dream Play* a seminal text in surrealism.

[22] *The Orestian Trilogy* is the only complete surviving Greek trilogy.

[23] Moliere is known for composing farces of manners in rhymed couplets. *Tartuffe* and *The Misanthrope* are representative works.

[24] Joe Orton popularized an aggressive modern farcical style. *Loot* and *What the Butler Saw* are two of his most popular plays.

[25] Amiri Baraka is the major figure in the Black Theatre renaissance of the 60's. *The Dutchman* is his seminal text.

[26] Henrik Ibsen is the most important proponent of the "well made play." *A Doll's House* is a representative text.

[27] Ntozake Shange made popular a genre called "choreopoem" with her Broadway hit play *For Colored Girls Who Have Considered Suicide When The Rainbow Is Enough*.

[28] Caryl Churchill is a modern absurdist writer who bends time and place in novel ways. *Cloud Nine* is a classic example.

[29] Sean "Diddy" Combs is a hip hop superstar known for aggressive "sampling" (i.e., recording sections from various songs and assembling them into a new piece of music].

techniques of numerous epochs to expand the limits of our imaginations.

The greatest writers have established the precedent. Brecht's[30] adaptation of the anonymous *Chalk Circle* points toward China. Wilder's[31] Theatre Without Walls pays homage to his experiences in Japan. Performers walking into a sacred area and assuming character speaks directly to Persian/Indian influences on Peter Shaffer's *Equus*.

The oddest factor in the philosophy of anti-intellectualism among authors is the inconsistency of its application. It is conceded that Terence[32] and Plautus[33] borrowed reverently from Greek models. *The Poetics*[34] acknowledges its use of Sophocles as a standard of dramatic excellence and has influenced generations of artists with its ideas of unity and catharsis. Ancient myths like Phaedra and Helen have been retold by dramatists of every era. Clearly only incompetent authors do not borrow from the greatness that surrounds them.

Our challenge, therefore, is to accept inspiration from peers and predecessors yet not plagiarize. The former

---

[30] Bertolt Brecht wrote *The Caucasian Chalk Circle*.

[31] Thornton Wilder's unusual style for *Our Town* was inspired by a trip to the Orient.

[32] Terence Afer, a Roman slave whose literary abilities so impressed and enriched his owners that he was set free.

[33] Plautus was the only credible rival to Terence for the title of greatest Roman writer of comedy.

[34] Aristotle's *The Poetics* is an analysis of the dramatic process and its effect on audiences utilizing *Oedipus Rex* by Sophocles as the model for a perfect play.

implies an insightful analysis of a work of art then the application of its rules to a contemporary project. Plays have quoted passages from earlier works. They have retold the same story in a new epoch or genre. Authors have penned sequels and prequels, revisited a subject from the perspective of a different character and so on ad infinitum. All are acts of creation practicable only because the writer was "studied."

Without an intellectual foundation we are in danger of repetition and blind to our greatest inspirations.

***

"What goes up eventually flies."
journal entry 1/20/80

ALIVE AND WELL
AND SPEAKING IN VERSE

One of the pleasures of my early adulthood was to walk the streets of Manhattan listening to Philip Hayes Dean share his theories of drama. By far the most memorable of all the ideas was his observation that dialogue was misnamed.

"It's poetry!" He explained that we write and rewrite our words. We construct and refine patterns of metaphors. We cut and add to make a satisfying aural landscape. "It's just blank verse."

August Wilson's country characters explode into convoluted, colorful, symbol-laden stories at the slightest provocation. Danton, as conceived by Georg Buchner, announces from the Bastille in the shadow of the Guillotine that "we're villains and angels, geniuses and boneheads all in one body...." Musicals disguise their poetry by renaming it "lyrics" when in reality it's only dialogue metered and set to melody.

For a time the argument was that poetry impeded drama. The unnaturalness of meter and rhyme was believed to clash with the demands of modern realism.

Even without embracing the philosophy of Philip Hayes Dean, one can debunk the anti-poets. Examples like *Richard III, Oedipus Rex, Signifying Monkey* and *Junebug Jabbo Jones* each capture in verse a passion every bit as vibrant as Tennessee Williams' Stanley Kowalski or David Mamet's Buffalo men.

My own explorations of verse, inspired by the lyricism of writers like Edmond Rostand,[35] Ed Bullins[36] and Ntozake Shange, began first as "high prose." This is a metaphor-laden genre that is rhythmic but not metered, poetic but not rhymed.

The Stalking Horse transported my observations of Harlem streetlife to a fictitious east African hunter/gatherer society. This setting excused the creation of a hybrid language that services both the drama and a heightened sense of style.

```
    "Oh that I were the spirit to
possess her. Surely it is a pleasure
worth several deaths but why does
```

---

[35] Edmond Rostand, a French dramatist, best known for his play *Cyrano de Bergerac.*

[36] Ed Bullins (*In The Wine Time*) was among a powerful group of playwrights who gave voice to and energized the Black revolutionary theatre movement in the late 60's and early 70's.

```
she move me? Her face is fair, her
figure firm, no single feature of
note does she possess. Neither has
she power to excite nor invite yet
she enraptures me and in the arms of
others my thoughts to her escape."
```

This language, if the play's conventions are not disbelieved, functions like realism despite its contrived quality. In fact, high prose serves to more passionately express emotion than photographic realism. Somehow the expanded vocabulary when fettered to a credible dramatic mooring allows the author to plunge deeper into the emotional truth of a moment.

Here is revealed the true timeless appeal of verse. Handled appropriately it unshackles the imagination of an author to unabashedly speak the most passionate secret truths of a character. Cyrano's eloquent rejection of pandering art justifies its lofty language and speaks the tortured soul of the disfigured swordsman. Othello sans poetic expressions of his "cause" would likely be a cautionary tale of domestic abuse.

It is surprising that so few authors embrace rhyme and meter when one considers the dramatic benefits. It appears that the short-lived "well-made play" movement has waged a successful campaign against versification and stylized language.

Certainly plot and dialogue had become dominated by contrivances at the time of Zola.[37] European scholars and writers had grown so enamored of the past that their own creations were often stilted and self-conscious.

Also, artists were commissioned throughout the continent by an elite disconnected from the creative process. These kings and nobles used whim and political agenda alternately to reinforce sometimes irrational and often ineffective dramatic choices. Both Wole Soyinka[38] and Augusto Boal[39] address this phenomenon at length; therefore herein we will instead devote our attentions to analyzing the emerging new verse.

There are no rules, only tactics. One useful approach to stylized dialogue is to construct each character's verse scheme as an independently functioning cycle. The advantage gained is that it becomes possible to maintain rigid verse rhythms that play like traditional dialogue except during the uninterrupted speeches of a single character.

---

[37] Emile Zola, French novelist and playwright, an important example of the literary school of naturalism. He became a major figure in the political liberalization of France with his publication of *J'Accuse,* condemning France's anti-Semitic treatment and subsequent jailing of Alfred Dreyfus.

[38] Nigerian playwright, Nobel Literature Laureate 1986, Soyinka was jailed for his political activism as a strong voice against Nigerian government oppression of Biafran citizens, and was released only through intense international pressure.

[39] Brazilian Workers' Party (PT) activist, playwright, director, theorist, teacher and founder/ inventor of a vast international movement, the Theatre of the Oppressed, established in the early 1970s. Oppression, according to Boal, is when one person is dominated by the monologue of another and has no chance to reply.

Last Call[40] utilizes this device. Barkeep and Young Lad speak in similar meters but with the accents altered. This serves to suggest different world-views. The tired, gruff, alehouse owner has lost the bounce of his young friend. Meanwhile, the mysterious old man has a completely different cadence and structure.

All three coexist wholly independent of one another. The poetry, therefore, only pushes its way to the foreground in moments of passion. Monologues, stories, speeches and harangues are the instances when someone in this world speaks uninterrupted, thus allowing the verse to identify itself. Those same moments of drama are so emotionally charged that we become lost in objective and excuse the contrivance of language.

Scott Miller, former artistic director of Children's Theatre of Charlotte, offered the single most useful piece of advice pertaining to poetry that any author could receive. When I explained that I intended to write the history of the King's Mountain battle of the War for American Independence as a project in verse, he warned, "Don't be bound by the verse."

Audiences tend toward collective, intuitive response. Verse at best is a subliminal pattern of language. If the dramatic moment ever is contradicted by the lyric structure, then an author must be free to abandon anything superfluous. There is no rule that requires an entire play to be perfectly metered. By the time one's work has been analyzed that microscopically, it is already successful.

---

[40] Reproduced in SECTION FOUR of this volume.

There are also innumerable creative reasons for shattering the extant verse structure. War, for example, is unpoetic in *Mountain*. All of the combatants meet on a battlefield littered with prose. In a similar way slaves exist outside the versification of the play. As the great grandson of an emancipated Virginia slave, I find nothing lyrical in the institution.

Writing verse requires making conscious rules and embracing exceptions. The more consistent the overall structure then the more actors and directors can lean on it for textual interpretations. There are moments in *Mountain*, for example, wherein someone's anger inspires him or her to prose. There are moments when shock breaks the meter causing a character to begin a new stanza without completing the last. Traitors and spies speak in slightly altered versions of the clans they attempt to mimic. Et cetera.

Each page of a verse play offers more choices with which to define the theatrical world. Most importantly, it challenges both audience and author to make meaning through analysis of style. The way an idea is rendered can reveal as much as any other aspect of the communication. Do, for example, Kings speak a different language from soldiers? Women from men? Children from adults?

Our choices are what reveal our souls. For writers, the opportunity to create an intricately considered verbal landscape inspires our best efforts.

The greater the challenge, the greater the victory.

***

*"How do I continue caring
yet somehow keep from going mad?"
journal entry 8/23/93*

BEST FOOT FORWARD

Robert Maurice Riley, a talented poet and playwright best known for the musical *Fixed*, once told a story about a child he encountered near Manhattan's historic Riverside Church. The young man had a series of pen and ink drawings glued to bits of cardboard on exhibit beside the church fence. Portraits, landscapes, superheroes and abstracts from his prepubescent mind were each selling for $2, three for $5.

Taken as a whole the body of work displayed "a lot more attitude than ability," but Robert was moved by the enterprise of this young artist and wanted to encourage his efforts through the purchase of a work.

Driven by this aim, Robert asked the child, "Which one is your best?" The young man did not hesitate for an instant before pointing to the half-done creation on his pad. This new drawing appeared in no obvious way different from the completed works already on display, but the profundity of the response was not lost on the poet.

Life can rob our labors of their joy. Or maybe it is more accurate to say that the necessities of survival can blind us to the Dionysian spirit of theatrical art.

The very best of our efforts are invariably born from the liberating abandon that occurs when we write from passion and unfettered imagination. Often the result is a producer's nightmare, but to do less is to risk smothering the child who sits sketching beside the wrought-iron fence of the church in our soul.

> *It is not happenstance that the works we labor to create are called "plays."*

***

"Live bravely, it is the only long life."
journal entry 4/19/92

WHEN I PICK UP MY PEN[41]

A short while ago I received an excited call from Scott Miller, former artistic director of Children's Theatre of Charlotte, North Carolina. Jack Beasley, retiring theatre reviewer for the *Charlotte Leader*, had devoted a sizable portion of his final season summary to explain why he considered my play, *Stranger On The Bus*, the best work of the year.

Scott's elation arose from a sense of vindication. During the three years of interviews and research that culminated in this Brechtian play, both the project and its producer [Scott] were subject to frequent attacks. At one particularly contentious juncture, Scott's judgment and job had become subject to review by a board of directors that was not in large part committed to the project or his continued tenure.

---

[41] This is an article that first appeared in the fall 1998 issue of *First Draft*, the Philadelphia Dramatists' Center (PDC) newsletter.

Despite enormous personal risk, Scott championed the literary process through three separate visionings of this play and one dozen drafts. His rare courage should be praised by every author and patron who suffers the banality of so-called "mainstream" theatre.

More importantly, the travail and triumph of this project scream of the need for a renegotiation of the relationship between artists and society. As Billie sings, "God bless the child...."

Our best work is invariably controversial. In order for creative and commercial interests of writers to be nurtured, we must exercise greater control over the presentation and development of plays. This is an agenda of Philadelphia Dramatists' Center (PDC) as we prepare for the challenges of this new millennium.

Resources for the successful completion of competent work should be available to all *practicing* writers. We need to control the scheduling of all the developmental stages from concept through completed text.

In order to achieve that end, we must establish what Jerry Givenish[42] called a "constellation of development activity." We should involve ourselves in direct negotiations with underutilized and alternative sites around the city. In this way PDC (or any organized theatre artists for that matter) can nurture the creation of writer-run venues for rehearsals, readings and showcase presentation. The greatest danger to the success of this empowering initia-

---

[42] Jerry Givenish was founder of the Painted Bride Arts Center in Philadelphia, which has served as a model for arts presenting organizations worldwide.

tive is vanity. "Authors" are driven by ego and avarice whereas "writers" pursue the successful exploration of a literary idea.

The former attitude will lead to competition among ourselves for showcase opportunities. The latter ideal will result in a collaboration to collectively improve our abilities and influence contemporary thought with our creativity.

John Burbage[43] said, "I was not put upon this earth to collect money." Translating that into twenty-first century language means that there are one hundred better ways to earn a buck than by writing plays. The unalterable truth of the matter is that every one of us hopes to write something that is profound, entertaining and moving.

"When I pick up my pen I am immortal."
Anonymous

PDC at its best can be an oasis in the wilderness of commercial forces and hidden agendas that threaten to suck the life out of contemporary theatre. By committing ourselves to excellence and creating an atmosphere of analysis rather than criticism, we will succeed both at unlocking our individual potentials and attracting the attention of the international community of theatre.

What are you writing on the walls of time?
***

---

[43] James Burbage, the famed British Shakespearean actor of the mid–sixteenth century.

*"Where one begins decides the heroes
and the villains."
journal entry 2/2/93*

ARTIST AS SENTINEL

Dr. Jack Nelson, former Graduate School Provost at Temple University, offered an inspired explanation of the place of affirmative action in American society. His analysis is equally applicable to the continuing national debate over the continuation of the National Endowment of the Arts program.

Contemporary philosophers differentiate between justice and morality. The former is a legal concept based upon ideas of fairness. The latter is a social or spiritual conclusion arising from either divine mandates or a conception of the greater good.

Simply put, it is foolish and dangerous to debate moral issues in legal terms. The justifications for social programs should be based exclusively on images of the world as we would like it to be.

If a nexus of historical/economic conditions have resulted in continuing high crime and unemployment among ethnic urban communities, then it is in the interest of society to change the situation. If universities need to attract greater numbers of non-white students, then increasing the representation of those ethnicities on faculties addresses that desired result. It remains unfair but morally sound[44].

Art, like affirmative action, should be assessed and supported based upon its relationship to the aesthetic best society. Are we served by diverse images and complex or conflicting styles and statements? Do challenging, even incendiary, creations inspire the most instructive public debates?

If the answer is, "Yes," then we must conspire to make conditions that encourage the development of brave work. This means funding artists rather than specific creations. An artist must be able to risk failure in order to pursue the most stimulating successes.

Individuals in North Carolina may quite naturally be offended by a sacred icon photographed in a urine-filled Mason jar. Robert Serrano's creation has frequently been cited as evidence of the worst in public art. In truth, however, his bold image best represents the necessity for courage and blind support of creativity.

---

[44] Employment quotas and race-based incentives may be unjust and simultaneously morally sound.

Firstly, no one denies his preeminence in the world of photography. The issue was never his enviable proficiency but rather questions of decency.

Secondly, an artist can never know the impact of a work until it is presented to an informed public. The same conservative constituency objected to "Angels in America" and "Six Degrees of Separation." This doesn't invalidate their opinions but does reveal that the Bible Belt measures of artistic efficacy are founded in issues of content rather than craft (unlike the artistic community and the lessons of history).

Thirdly, and most importantly, the very thing that has made this oft-cited image objectionable is its most compelling argument. The idea of a religious icon, a piece of metal and wood, being regarded as sacred is the foundation of a two-thousand-year-old theological debate. Golden calves et al., the examination of the cross as potentially a "graven image" is enormously relevant and of particular service to the most reverent Christians in American society.

This is how art serves society....

Artists stand like Ibsen's sentinel[45] peering around a bend and warning an often antagonistic hoard of an approaching, unperceived danger.

***

---

[45] An allusion to the climatic speech in *An Enemy Of The People* by Henrik Ibsen.

*"All roads lead home but some have
less potholes."
journal entry 1/28/94*

NOTES FROM A PRACTICING WRITER

You have to keep a journal. It is the compost heap
that nourishes the flowers of your imagination. It is
the repository of half-baked ideas. It is an unedited
safe house for observations of life and oneself. It is
the surest defense against literary lethargy and the
ultimate unerring guarding of one's self image.

The following notes are excerpts from decades of
journal entries. They accompany my growth from a
spindly Afro'ed kid in a New England prep school
through to a graying father of two struggling always
to turn the lead of words into the gold of ideas.

The entries that I have selected represent observations
that carried me through each of the sections of this book.
Some are themes of plays, others the thoughts that provided direction or solace throughout a difficult career. Many
are conclusions and questions that crystallized into my

idea of art. My hope is that authors will hear echoes and affirmations of their own journey toward beauty.

"Solutions work better than assigning blame."

4/2/98

"Many writers seem to write clever works that say nothing. They ask no questions and offer no answers."

4/18/98

"Every life has cause for joy and despair. The secret is to take strength from the former to endure the rest."

5/25/98

"A flower's just a weed that someone loves."

5/5/98

"The greatest gift of all is discipline."

5/7/98

"Sometimes I have so many ideas that I can't think."

7/10/98

"Everything isn't always for the best, but we can make the best of anything."

10/23/98

"Much of all writing is purely intuitive. The trick is to fill your mind with options so that the unconscious can function unimpeded while the conscious mind is quick to recognize the emerging structures."

10/29/98

"To learn is to enter into a thing and feel its soul."

3/5/94

"To hide a sore is to make it fester."

2/26/94

"The new becomes common so we are not wise to rest success upon the new. Instead make the common that will endure..."

7/31/85

"Dennis Moritz[46] talked about 'speech strategies.' I need to be more conscious of identifying them in real people then putting them into my characters."

2/10/94

"Few things are less impressive than someone trying to impress."

2/9/94

---

[46] Literary manager of Theatre Double, author of *Quick, Fast And In A Hurry*.

"In San Diego at the Pickwick Hotel. I couldn't reach Terri[47] so I'm making the most of it until I pick up a rental car tomorrow morning. I feel impelled to write so as to justify the expense of a room but at the same time I'm exhausted. Certainly the trip has introduced me to new characters. I don't know that they'll appear in my writing but it can't hurt. The 'bus poor' spitting tobacco into soda cans are different from my usual circles. There also is a healthy mix with blonde college types, gray-haired Wicas, Chicanos, Mexicans, Indians and all. Does it make me a better writer? Who knows? I need to see it all."

12/29/93

"The less you want, the more you have."

2/11/94

"There's nothing worth regretting that I can't forget."

3/16/94

"Some nights make day seem near never to come."

3/12/94

"No gift is ever so welcome as love."

3/11/94

"Nothing lies more convincingly than evidence."

8/18/94

---

[47] Terri Shockley is my wife.

"Hope is a bed of nails."

10/9/94

"It is far easier to avoid a problem than it is to solve one."

11/26/94

"In revision I should always look to add a taboo..."

6/13/95

"If life is a mine field then I must have awfully large feet."

5/10/95

"Short Eyes[48] calls to me. I need to write a play of stunning clarity. This also says that I need to write something with such power. Bobos[49] is a funky trip to OZ. 30 Seconds of Silence is closer to the real deal but I need a full-length work that drips menstrual blood."

4/17/93

"I need to become aware of pacing in poetry just as I am in theatre. The changes in rhythm and meter should facilitate and enhance changes in meaning and mood. Move the reader through the river of words."

11/6/93

---

[48] Jose Pinero's gritty prison drama about a child molester.

[49] Award winning urban opera by James McBride and Ed Shockley that premiered at the American Music Theatre Festival. Part of the Lincoln Center library, New York. Music Theatre video collection.

"How will I make a new poetry? Redundancy is the enemy. Is it enough to sing new ideas with the same words or must I always reform my structures as well as themes? No, the structures are more important than the themes."

4/6/93

"Today Bob Hedley [50] argued that we write our ideas and greatness is thrust upon us. It sounds great but I don't buy it. The ideas with scope are clear even if I fail to execute the vision. The Graveyard *has a potential that exceeds* Bedlam Moon. *The trick is to be brave enough to swing for the back wall."*

4/30/92

"Use what you know, write what you feel."

4/21/93

***

---

[50] Robert Hedley, founder of the Iowa Playwrights Lab, former Theatre Department Chair, Temple University.

SECTION THREE

THE CAREER OF PLAYWRITING

*"The best hours
Of the best days
Of our best years
Are spent working
So choose well."
journal entry 3/22/95*

"If I can find a way to live and write,
I will have lived well."
journal entry 12/9/80

PURSUING COMMISSIONS

A theatrical commission is the awarding of a mandate by an artistic director, producer or actor to create a work for hire. This is usually accompanied by a guarantee of production and financial remuneration.

"It's not who you know, it's not what you know, it's who you know who likes you."

Robert Maurice Riley

Mr. Riley has expounded the single most important factor in securing commissions. Personal charisma is the "x factor" in this equation, but there are certain tactics that will better position any competent author to be considered for projects.

Commissions can be obtained at any stage in one's career. The requirements are a bit of luck and the ability to convince a producing professional to trust that you will deliver a complete and competently crafted script in a timely fashion.

First and foremost, it is necessary to attract the attention of the producing agency. Typically this is done by having a series of scripts rejected... encouragingly. *"We love the writing but...," "the subject...," "at this time...," "too large...," "too small...," "too too...."*

The second or third encouraging rejection can be followed by the request for a conference with the artistic director or his/her representative. Sending *periodic* career updates in the interim is a good idea. Readings, productions, contests, etc.

A typical conversation would begin, "You've been very encouraging in your responses to my writing and I'd like to discuss several works in development to see if one of my planned ideas peaks your interest." Once that stop sign is passed, the conversation allows the question, "Perhaps there's a subject you're interested in that I'd be willing to explore?"

Every artistic director has a pet project she has secretly carried in her heart. Linda Hartzell at Seattle Children's Theatre inspired my adaptation of Mildred D. Taylor's *Roll Of Thunder Hear My Cry.* Carl Clay, founder of New York's Black Spectrum Theatre Company, longed to explore the history of blacks in Queens. Bernard Havard of Philadelphia's Walnut Street Theatre still waits for a talented dramatization of Fannie Kemble's abolitionist diary.

Once a topic is posed, it is best to take a few days to research the subject.

A wise practice is to develop a "point of attack" before accepting the assignment. This may ultimately change, but the timely delivery of a clever approach to the subject both reassures the theatre and insures that the collaboration will be amicable. For example, the history of blacks in Queens, New York initially did not capture my interest. Research led me to frame an autobiographical play set inside the conscious and subconscious mind of a writer pursuing a possibly fictitious memory of an event that occurred in Queens. Both the theatre's mission and the artist's mission must be satisfied.

DO'S AND DON'TS

- *Do get as much time as possible to complete each draft.*
- *Do get an outline approved before creating a text.*
- *Do feel free to borrow classical structures or plagiarize yourself.*
- *Do plan and contract for six to ten drafts.*
- *Do create a specific image of the target audience. (Bible belt drama uses different language than San Francisco.)*
- *Do have fun.*

- *Don't try to please everyone.*
- *Don't share early drafts with a large group at the producing theatre.*
- *Don't lose the drama in a mountain of facts.*
- *Don't be intimidated or sell yourself short.*
- *Don't be afraid to create in genres other than realism.*

Ultimately every commissioned play should be one that you would have written anyway. A work for hire must still be a labor of love; otherwise, the intense and immutable pressure of deadlines will make life miserable. The financial incentive entices you to alter the order of your creations, not the content. This is what separates the artist from the artisan.

Gnothi seuton **(Know thyself).**

***

"The sky is not so far away as it seems."
journal entry 8/22/83

MAPPING A CAREER

Early in my high school career at St. Paul's School in Concord, New Hampshire,[51] I acted in a student play by "Chip" Lamason. Only a single line of dialogue remains with me from the experience:

"A penetrating glimpse into the obvious."

The three observations that I prepare to offer here could easily be designated "Lamason observations." This does not mean, however, that they are any less true or effective.

"EVERYTHING IS AN ALPHABET"

By reducing any activity to a series of small tasks, then one achieves a complex result. You will find this equally true in physical and intellectual pursuits.

---

[51] see *Black Ice* by Lorene Cary for an account of our years at St. Paul's School.

Boxers study tapes of Kid Gavilan and catalogue the conditions where his infamous "bolo punch" surprised an embarrassed opponent. Basketballers study Dennis Rodman's techniques and boost their rebounding averages. Financiers examine how billionaire Donald Trump survived near bankruptcy and thereby rescue their own failing businesses. "A penetrating glimpse into the obvious."

At the start of my playwriting career, I searched for some successful author whose actions I might emulate in hopes of achieving corresponding results.

Help with creative challenges was readily available in the works of masters both ancient and contemporary. More difficult to unearth was someone informed about the business of theatre with the accompanying generosity to prepare me for the complexities that accompany life in the world of professional theatre.

Playing varsity basketball at Columbia University exposed me to several theatre impresarios. Ron Kapon[52] was an investor in the Broadway hit *Robber Bridegroom* and introduced me to Liz McCann.[53] The late Mo Septee[54] had a daughter at Barnard College; but neither he, nor director Aaron Frankl[55], nor acclaimed actor Laurence Luckinbill[56] could address the particular obstacles facing

---

[52] Writer and wine expert who invests heavily in and champions the arts.

[53] Producer with Nellie Nugent of *Dracula* & *Gin Game*.

[54] Successive producer and presenter of road shows.

[55] Director and author of *How to Write a Broadway Musical*.

[56] Mr. Luckinbill directed Bertolt Brecht's *Gallileo* in the Oppenheimer laboratory during a hiatus from the Broadway premiere of *The Shadow Box*.

a poor kid from South Philadelphia as he assaulted the Great White Way.

Most enticing among all of these intimate strangers was Melvin Van Peebles. His eclectic career as film producer[57], actor, recording artist, playwright[58], journalist, et al., while battling the stereotypes of a racist society, identified him as the perfect advisor for this son of a plumber.

I got his phone number from directory assistance and called him from a New York subway platform: "Babes and fools...." Instead of being offended, he invited me to his home and shared the story of his early career.

He had wanted to be a journalist but had no recognized credentials in an industry that did not at that time welcome blacks. Harlem, however, was electric with news. Malcolm,[59] Martin,[60] Stokely,[61] A. Phillip Randolph,[62] the Panthers, Vinette Carroll,[63] Baraka and a plethora of lesser known activists, agitators and rebels

---

[57] *Sweet Sweetback's Baadasssss Song* is acknowledged as the spark that ignited the sixties black film renaissance.

[58] *Ain't Supposed To Die A Natural Death* was an early 1970s Broadway success.

[59] Malcolm X, assassinated minister for the Nation of Islam, formally known as El Hajj Malik el Shabazz.

[60] The Reverend Doctor Martin Luther King, Jr., assassinated Civil Rights leader.

[61] Stokely Carmichael, leader of the Student Non-violent Coordinating Committee (SNCC), became a Pan-Africanist and changed his name to Kwame Toure.

[62] Leader and first president of the Sleeping Car Porters Union, also one of the organizers of the 1963 March on Washington.

[63] Historic producer/director of *Don't Bother Me I Can't Cope, Your Arms Too Short To Box With God*, et al.

were incessantly redefining the place of blacks in the city and nation.

It was an environment not wholly welcoming or even healthy for white newsmen, and Mr. Van Peebles exploited it by volunteering to cover, for free, any event that the paper chose to assign him.

His only condition was that his name be placed on the byline of any article that was accepted for publication.

After months of this pro bono labor, Mr. Van Peebles went to a cross-town rival news organization, showed his clippings and asked them to beat his current salary. The lesson:

"NOBODY TURNS DOWN A VOLUNTEER."

My own early career illustrates the application of this principle. Space is precious in New York. Theatre space is to die for. As a student at Columbia University, the various state-of-the-art facilities were available to anyone who could type a proposal.

Kuumba Edwards, Hammond Jerome Briscoe, III, Richard Claytor, Margaret Cesare Thompson and Clifton Smith started a black theatre company during the fall of my freshman year. Together we parlayed those resources into an introduction into New York's Black Theatre society.

Ntozake Shange, George Faison, Morgan Freeman, Richard Wesley, Reginald Van Johnson, Debbie Allen, June Jordan, Gwendolyn Brooks and on and on... All became accessible by the volunteering of our space and labor. National Black Theatre, the late Roger Furman's

New Heritage Theatre, Henry Street Settlement, Negro Ensemble Company—these theatres and more opened their doors, hearts and memories to the hungry young volunteers from that white college on Morningside Heights.

The three most important relationships for me personally were Garland Lee Thompson, Robert Maurice Riley[64] and Richard Wesley.

Garland brought the Broadway-bound production of *Inacent Black* from Frank Silvera Writers' Workshop to our campus. I followed it from the readings at his small Harlem space, through our Columbia Showcase run to Billie Holliday Theatre and its brief Broadway stint. Along the way I learned the business of theatre and was introduced to the exhaustive revision process that resulted in my first record-setting production.

Richard Wesley, being only a few years my senior, modeled the life of a successful writer for my consideration. Attending shows with him, discussing his plays and films, his militant early work and mainstream current voice confirmed the path of my creative life.

Robert Maurice Riley came to Columbia University to direct *From Okra to Greens*, a work in progress by Ntozake Shange. His professionalism and precision became the model for how I have carried myself throughout my career. Moreover, the collaborations that began with

---

[64] Robert Maurice Riley, the playwright/poet of the early 1980's off Broadway hit, *Fixed*.

volunteerism have each grown into lasting friendships, a marvelous fringe benefit of the Van Peebles philosophy.

As you pursue a career, take heed of the invaluable advice offered by the ever-acerbic Philip Hayes Dean. After an SRO performance of *Bessie Smith: Empress of the Blues*, he discussed my work with Howard Moore.[65] Mr. Dean's comment was, "He needs to go somewhere and learn how to write."

Being intimately acquainted with Mr. Dean's fine work allowed me not to take offense at his assessment of the children's play that started my career. *The Owl Killer*, *Sty of the Blind Pig* and the astounding *Paul Robeson* (which I attended alone as a twenty-first birthday present to myself) were all clearly superior in craft and scope to my simple expressionistic musical.

Margaret Cesare Thompson[66] reiterated the same message in her gentle but equally forceful style after I appeared on some cable talk show with David Henry Hwang.[67] "Ed," she said, "you're in danger of becoming an author."

The final advice as you prepare for a career is, therefore, remember always:

---

[65] Author of the play *Don't Call Me Man*, which starred the late jazz great Betty Carter.

[66] Author of *The True History of Paradise*.

[67] The equally young author of *M Butterfly* whose first hit, *Dance and the Railroad* was running at the Public Theatre.

"THE PLAY'S THE THING."

There are easier ways to make money than writing for the theatre. All of us enter it to speak the truth as we know it. This focus allows you to enjoy the vicissitudes of an unstable industry and fulfill your promise as an author.

"Authors come and go; writers are forever."

***

"I'm often disgusted but never discouraged."
journal entry 4/27/86

TWO ROADS

More years ago than I care to admit, one of my father's girlfriends defined the two life paths open to an artist. I've long since forgotten the woman's name (he had many girlfriends), but her words have affected all of my life.

By day this nameless woman worked writing grants or something corporate. She had a young son and needed medical, dental and money for Dr. Denton P.J.'s. Her passion, however, was weaving. She composed beautiful canvasses of wool as an expression of her creative spirit.

The works were pricey because of the enormous time investment. Still, she had met with modest success, periodically receiving a commission for a wall-sized hanging from a bank or business. Occasionally, a person of wealth would purchase one of the smaller works to adorn a mansion wall.

Upon learning that I was interested in art, this kind woman described the crossroads facing each of us:

> *1. Either we assume a career then practice art as a hobby,*
>
> OR
>
> *2. We accept mindless labor, that leaves our imaginations and bodies free to focus constantly on the problems of creation.*

The first path offers material security (hence we'll call it the "high road"). Many people cannot concentrate on art when the rent is not paid. Careers, therefore, with long vacations like school teaching or early retirements like the military, leave ample time to satisfy both the muse and dunners.[68]

The alternate path involves usually low-paying seasonal labor (hence its designation as the "low road"). Temp work, waiting tables, security, etc., are jobs rather than careers. Such employment requires little more than punctuality and allows one to reserve the best labor hours for art.

Each path has advantages and drawbacks. Careers tend to grow. Responsibilities escalate until frequently all of the very best years have been sacrificed to the Gods of Commerce. The economic security of the high road does free one to create without deference to the marketplace, but whether this is a blessing or curse is a complex question.

---

[68] Bill collectors

The low road keeps an artist both figuratively and physically hungry. Art is an escape from the drudgery of work in this scenario. One's hopes for a better life are transferred to pen or quill or brush. Frequently artists produce greater volumes of work in this perpetual desperation because there are fewer distractions and intense urgency.

The starving artist cliché can grow tiresome very quickly. It attacks one's self esteem. It requires perfect health since America has no National Health Care. The artist must sacrifice creature comforts and must often postpone key aspects of life like family, retirement preparation, advanced study, etc.

Artists of distinction have emerged from both approaches. Anton Chekhov was a medical doctor. Langston Hughes was supported by demanding patrons. Georg Buchner was a scientist. Alice Childress cleaned houses early in her career. The goal is to choose the path that suits one's character.

Two principal questions determine the direction one should go.

Firstly, what is your relationship to the material world? There are sandals-and-jeans folk and others who are allergic to lunchmeat. Some artists easily ignore bills and smells or even use them as inspirations. Other artists cannot work until the right place and time. "Know thyself" applies to the writer as well as the creation.

Secondly, why do you write? It is amazing how few authors address this most fundamental question. The answer defines what one writes and what talents one is able to exploit. For example, a writer who does this because it's fun can compose advertising copy and live well. A writer who thinks the spirit of God seizes her and directs her pen will not cheapen that miracle by describing the newest drip coffee maker.

In my own life I've chosen the low road again and again. Initially, during the pre-Reagan economy, I was able to work a few months, pay rent ahead then quit and write nonstop until the wolves began to scratch at the door. I ate at the numerous New York gallery openings and public receptions. A fire gutted the middle floors of my Harlem walk-up so I lived rent-free in the condemned building until my first hit show. Thereafter, I traveled to whatever city produced one of my creations and found work at theatres or gave lectures, etc.

The lifestyle is alternately described as a "trapeze act" or "living out in the cold." I stopped counting jobs after the forty-second because my stint as a theatre gypsy began. My relationship to writing didn't allow me to capitalize on opportunities to write slide shows, advertising copy, industrial films or anything that I would not be comfortable calling my last work. Every "no" makes your flat another degree colder.

The best part of this journey is that I've walked a mile in many shoes. By viewing society alternately from the perspectives of various classes—author looking through a tinted limousine window, squatter in a burned-out building, bank teller, street corner performer—I have been taught to empathize and to see into the conditions that shape the choices of a variety of people.

Also, without any alternative but the success of a play to free me from oppressive poverty, I have been inspired to my best creations. Few lifestyles would have resulted in six-dozen plays, six screenplays, two novels, a box of musical compositions, et al. I'm forced to look hard and truthfully at my writing or risk starvation.

Undoubtedly this life choice has also made me prematurely gray. It may ultimately claim my teeth from postponed or neglected dental care. It has allowed my two children to be born on public assistance, and it has taken twenty-one years to repay my undergraduate loans. All this and I am a model of the successful American playwright.

My professional career began in 1981. Fresh out of Columbia University, I won the Audelco Award for best musical production with a record-setting premiere of *Bessie Smith: Empress Of The Blues*. In 1982, the same play began a year-long off-off-Broadway run in the Windy City and was chosen "Year's Best" by *Chicago Magazine*. In 1983, the play reopened off-Broadway in Chicago starring Odetta and Jean Dushon. *The Strange Career of John Hopewell* (1984) received the Lorraine Hansberry Award. *The Stalking Horse* (1985) won the American Minority Playwrights' Contest. *Stranger on the Bus* was nominated both for "best play" and "best new play" (winning the latter) in Charlotte, North Carolina. *Bobos* (co-authored with James McBride) broke the ten-year-old box office record at the American Music Theatre Festival (which had premiered Duke Ellington's *Queenie Pie* and *X* by Anthony Davis). It then went on to win the Stephen Sondheim Award, the Richard Rodgers Award, yadda yadda yadda.

I offer this to give a truthful picture of the career of authors in the American theatre. In any given year less than fifty writers earn $25,000 in royalties from plays. It means that sanitation engineers live in nicer homes than playwrights who do not marry money or take the high road.

Personally, I chose the path that suited my character. What I have seen and done is priceless. What I have learned and shared is precious. What suffering and want have prodded me to become is enviable. Still, I wish I had seen more clearly the reality of the economics of theatre at the start. Maybe I would have bought savings bonds instead of those hip Chicago boots with my first royalty check.

Choose the right path for the right reasons.

***

*"Never burn your bridges
before you cross them."
journal entry 3/21/84*

THE BOX SELLS THE CEREAL

I completed my last year of undergraduate study in 1979 and lived a marvelously creative summer in a $135-per-month, two-room flat in Spanish Harlem. Days began with letter writing. A long hot bath and an exploration of some classic piece of literature followed. A simple breakfast. Intense writing. A bike ride to some comfortable Manhattan locale. More writing. Home for a shower, then a night in the Village or wherever life was bursting its buttons.

Out of this unique summer emerged *The Stalking Horse*. This complex drama exploring obsession in a fictitious East African village remains one of my best crafted plays, yet it initially received so many rejections that it ended up buried in a trunk in the back of my mother's third floor, walk-in closet for half a decade.

In the mid-eighties, electronic typewriters became affordable to the working poor. *The Stalking Horse* was then *retyped* on a Canon memory typewriter and again set loose on the world. This time, however, the play won the American Minority Playwrights' Contest.

The lesson is that "format counts." We wish it were otherwise but in our image-conscious society the box often sells the cereal.

We are then wise to type our scripts neatly without typographical errors. They must be securely bound in one of the three standard styles; Velo binding, spiral binding with plastic covers or manuscript cover. There should be a title page with author's name, address, e-mail, and phone number, agent information and professsional affiliations; a character page, page numbers centered at the bottom....

Beyond these technical basics there is an aesthetic series of presentation choices that position one's script to receive a favorable reading. "Giving it legs" is the metaphor that describes one's goal. It is the practice of finding something that causes a text to stand apart from the mass of unsolicited projects flowing into most American theatres.

Years ago I served as an intern at American Place Theatre in Manhattan. Among my duties was the task of assisting their literary manager, Cynthia Jennings.

On the wall of her office, there stood a row of scripts neatly filed on a suspended shelf. These represented the "priority reads." Our instructions were to read all of these first, then, if there was time remaining, examine the contents of a large desk drawer. Inside the drawer was a graveyard filled with dreams. These were the unsolicited manuscripts that received only the scraps of our attention.

Priority scripts were the agent submissions, selections of key theatre staff or associated directors, produced plays and authors whose names had caché of some sort. These works were all read cover-to-cover and summarized in thoughtful script reports, prepared so that intelligent responses could be communicated to the interested parties. This is the way that you want your script to be considered.

Successful play presentation requires an author to communicate some validating information about the text. "Winner of.." serves that function if there is a contest history. Quotes from a review are helpful with the article in its entirety included as an appendix. "Developed at..." informs the reader that dramaturgy has been performed on this work at a reputable establishment.

The best positioning of a script is to have direct contact with the theatre or producer. A query letter and synopsis, for example, can peak the interest of the literary manager and guarantee a warm read if they request the complete manuscript. (One is wise to include a stamped response card with the query.)

Directors or actors who have worked at the target theatre can access the priority theatre pile. Furthermore, these practicing artists are more often actively searching for projects to showcase their talents.

Public readings at developmental theatres are useful tools because they serve creative and career needs. Hearing the text reveals strengths and weaknesses. It supplies a barometer of audience interest. It also aligns actors and directors with your play.

Jon Dorf, online playwriting consultant for The Writer's Store in Los Angeles, has had remarkable success marketing works via the internet. There are writers' chat groups, theatrical billboards and theatre sites that simplify the query process.

If the work of the author is incomplete, then each of these activities becomes a detriment to one's career. First impressions are lasting impressions. Producers are looking to say, "No." They have more plays than they need. Additionally, they do not have to pay royalties for presenting all of the departed masters. Your play is a salmon swimming upstream, leaping waterfalls and dodging bear.

Be absolutely certain that your play is a strong fish
before getting into the water.

***

"The devil's not the only one buying souls."
journal entry 12/31/92

SIGN ON THE DOTTED LINE

You've written a stunning play. You've packaged it wisely. Production is being negotiated. Wait!!!

In the excitement of the long-awaited moment, it is easy to forget that, in this America, art is a business. The success of your play can tie you economically to a choreographer, director, music director, copyist, developmental theatre, commercial producer and several Equity actors for years to come. A moment of caution can avoid a lifetime of regret.

If there is good news in this affair, then it is this: people don't steal plays, they steal money. There is so little wealth in our industry and so many obstacles to success that the better class of crooks go to Hollywood, Nashville, Detroit, etc.

Everyone asks the author for everything. This is not a problem provided the author knows that it is okay to say, "No." The director wants a percentage of royalties for her insightful dramaturgical contributions. "No." A small theatre wants exclusive rights to mount your show before anywhere else on earth. "No." The producer wants to keep all profits from merchandizing. "No." Nicole Kidman wants to create the role of Mabel if she receives more stage time. "Well, maybe."

The Dramatist Guild of America is a marvelous arbitrator. Associate membership is currently $99 per year and they have standard theatre contracts for Broadway, off-Broadway and the new 99-seat contract[69]. If you use and register an approved Dramatist Guild contract, then the Guild will aggressively help resolve disputes that may arise.

Often plays are developed at venues that aren't covered by Guild guidelines. Many theatres big and small are not signatories. Even in these situations the Dramatists Guild model can help define what is a fair grant of rights and encumbrances. The trick is to know what is standard and what you want. Armed with that information any competent contract lawyer *using theatrical documents as models* can represent your interests.

Years ago, as a foolish kid, I copied contracts in New York University Law Library and assembled all of the clauses that were favorable to the writer. These documents actually earned me more than the Dramatist

---

[69] The physical theatre size and relationship to the Equity union define the production. 99 seats or less is off-off, 100–299 is off and 300 or more is Broadway when a commercial producer is involved. Special LORT (League of Regional Theatres) dispensations exist to support the activities of not-for-profit venues.

Guild minimums. It isn't a course of action that I would recommend but the practice of studying model contracts before signing anything is wise.

Theatre is a unique world that requires special considerations. The fact is theatrical lawyers—and most especially competent ones—are few and far between. The hourly rate of an accomplished barrister can quickly exceed the entire royalty of many productions. This combination of factors requires authors to know what is reasonable to ask for and practical to concede.

While I was working between shows at an East Side New York answering service, a fellow operator shared an interesting secret. Her mother worked at a midtown producing theater that was negotiating the rights to a hot new show. I was told in confidence that the producer would ask for any and everything as a matter of course. Authors frequently respond as if receiving ultimatums when in point of fact their plays were going to be produced whether these extravagant rights were surrendered or not.

All of this points to the necessity for arbitrators. An agent or business manager can ask for things that seem unreasonable in the mouth of an author. Their 10% will land you in a first class hotel with per diem expenses that include travel days and taxi refunds. More importantly, if the negotiations become acerbic, it is always possible to dismiss your proxy and begin again with knowledge of unassailable limits.

Information can equal success in the business of theatre. Cities with dramatist centers routinely sponsor free or low cost panels/workshops. In lieu of such opportunities, there are several fine books on the business of theatre including *The Seesaw Log*[70] and Dana Singer's comprehensive new examination of our industry.[71]

Whatever tactic one uses to develop business savvy, it is imperative to accept the reality that...

The facility of our art defines our place in history while our ability at business determines our place in society.

***

---

[70] William Gibson, author of *The Miracle Worker*, chronicles the painful journey from last line to Broadway opening of his play *Two For A Seesaw*. It is especially informative because it captures the power struggle of a star driven project.

[71] *Stage Writers Handbook: A Complete Business Guide for Playwrights, Composers, Lyricists and Librettists*, by Dana Singer, former head of the Dramatists Guild Legal Department, perhaps the greatest living authority on playwrights' rights.

SECTION FOUR

PLAYS & EXCERPTS

"I make no claim to perfection or perfect knowledge of my faults."
Journal entry 6/18/85

SUNSET JOHNSON

e. shockley

A SHORT PLAY BY
[Excerpted from RESERVATION ROAD]

N. 18th St.
Phila. PA 19140
Email: edshockley@edshockley.com
Website: edshockley.com

Representation: Mark Beigelman,
Kaufman, Feiner, Gilden, & Robbins,
777 Third Ave., 24th Floor, NY, NY 10017

Cast of CHARACTERS

FREDERICK "SUNSET" JOHNSON Black WWI vet recently returned

LILA DELOUISE White adolescent farmgirl

AT RISE: Late afternoon in a tree enclosed pasture. Lila enters chasing a butterfly. Sunset lights a cigarette.

                    LILA
Who that?

                    SUNSET
Who askin'?

                    LILA
What you doin' out here in the woods?

                    SUNSET
Havin' me a smoke and hidin' from my
daddy till plantin's done.

                    LILA
I'm duckin' spring slaughter.

                    SUNSET
And chasing butterflies.

                    LILA
Yeah.

                    SUNSET
You're a fast little thing.

                    LILA
I ain't that fast.

                    SUNSET
Bet you could beat me.

                    LILA
If I was of a mind to, maybe.

                  SUNSET
What might put a pretty girl like you of
a mind?

                    LILA
I don't know.

                  SUNSET
Maybe if I was a butterfly.

                    LILA
Maybe.

                  SUNSET
But would you know what to do with me
once you caught me?

                    LILA
I spect so.

                  SUNSET
You got to hold me tight so I don't slip
out.

                    LILA
Are we talkin' bout the same thing?

                  SUNSET
Spect so.

                    LILA
You're too fast for me.

                    SUNSET
I'll let you catch me.

                    LILA
I do believe you're getting fresh.

                    SUNSET
Just talkin' butterflies and running
fast.

                    LILA
Don't I know you?

                    SUNSET
Ain't likely with the crow.

                    LILA
You used to go to the cullered school
over on Reservation road.

                    SUNSET
Everybody round here cullered went to
that school.

                    LILA
You used to skinny dip down by the crossroads. I'd see you from the bus window.

                    SUNSET
You must come from money.

                    LILA
My uncle drove it.

                    SUNSET
That's convenient...How come you remember
me all these years?

                    LILA
It's...I can't say.

                    SUNSET
Suit yourself.

                    LILA
You used to always stand up still like a
statue with water dripping down your body
and everything out in the open and all.

                    SUNSET
And you remembered all these years?

                    LILA
It was the first time, oh God, I don't
believe I'm sayin' this.

                    SUNSET
Ain't a word got to leave this grove.

                    LILA
It's the first time I see'd a cullered's
thing.

                    SUNSET
You seen many more since?

                    LILA
Where would I get to do that?

                         SUNSET
A girl has ways.

                         LILA
I ain't studying nobody's thing, cullered
or white.

                         SUNSET
Glad to hear it.

                         LILA
Why zat?

                         SUNSET
If I was to take a liking to you then it'd
be extra special if I was the first and
only somebody you'd ever seen that way.

                         LILA
You shouldn't be talkin' to me like this.

                         SUNSET
Like what?

                         LILA
You know.

                         SUNSET
If I knowed I wouldn'tve asked.

                         LILA
You from round here same's me.

                         SUNSET
I'm from round lots of places.

LILA
You been hoboin'? That where you been
these last few years?

SUNSET
How you know how long I been gone?

LILA
You either been hoboin' or been in jail.

SUNSET
Naw, baby Jane.

LILA
That ain't my name.

SUNSET
What is?

LILA
I ain't sure I should tell you.

SUNSET
How come?

LILA
Cause I don't want you passing lies on me
to all your cullered friends.

SUNSET
I ain't had cause to lie on you.

LILA
And I ain't gonna give you cause neither.

                    SUNSET
So what are you gon' give me on this hot
afternoon?

                    LILA
I ain't gonna give you nothin' but my back.

                    SUNSET
You got a pretty back far as I can see.

                    LILA
You know what I mean.

                    SUNSET
Sure do.

                    LILA
Stop that.

                    SUNSET
What?

                    LILA
Twisting round everything I say till it's
dirty.

                    SUNSET
Seem to me like we was talkin' bout
butterflies and giving names.

                    LILA
You know what you meant.

                    SUNSET
What'd I mean?

                    LILA
I ain't got to say it.

                    SUNSET
Naw, baby Jane, you ain't got to do
nothin' 'cept shake your sugarbowl when
you walk.

                    LILA
Sunset Johnson, you stop gettin' fresh
with me.

                    SUNSET
You callin my name sweet how I like to
hear it and I'm thinkin' it's mighty
peculiar for this pretty girl to know how
long my train been gone and remember who
I am when I come back.

                    LILA
I hear your name around.

                    SUNSET
Around where?

                    LILA
Here and there.

                    SUNSET
And what they sayin' bout Sunset Johnson?

                    LILA
They saying you crazy in the head like
your daddy.

                    SUNSET
We out here havin' us a pleasant talk on
a summer day so don't go disrespectin' my
daddy.

                    LILA
I'm just repeating what they say.

                   SUNSET
I done spoke on it, baby Jane, now let it
lay.

                   (PAUSE)

                    LILA
Delilah.

                   SUNSET
Come again?

                    LILA
My name is Lila Delouise but folks took
to callin' me Delilah.

                   SUNSET
I bet they do.

                    LILA
You must be just off the county farm.

                   SUNSET
Why's that?

                    LILA
Cause you only think about one thing.

                   SUNSET
Seem like you doin' as much thinkin' as
me...I just got out the service.

                    LILA
You fought in the war?

                    SUNSET
When they let me.

                    LILA
No wonder you so crazy.

                    SUNSET
What's crazy 'bout a man talkin' to a
pretty girl on a summer day?

                    LILA
A cullered boy talkin' to a white woman?

                    SUNSET
A lonely man talkin' to a friendly girl.

                    LILA
I done heard you called a many things and
lonely ain't one of 'em.

                    SUNSET
Johnson don't regular let the sun set on
an empty bed; I ain't lying or denying.

                    LILA
A girl'd have to be a fool to go with a
fella like you.

                    SUNSET
There must be a powerful many fools run
from here all the way through Brownsville
and over up in Europe.

                    LILA
There must be.

                    SUNSET
And I bet you can't name one of 'em.

                    LILA
You like betting, don't you?

                    SUNSET
I like winning.

                    LILA
What you trying' to win here?

                    SUNSET
A taste of heaven by the name of Lila
Delouise.

                    LILA
We both more like to catch hell.

                    SUNSET
Maybe, but, I done picked a great big
willow tree got leaves hang down almost
to the ground. When you get up in there
it be dark like night and cool as a creek
side. I done found that spot and said to
myself, this here is made for thrill.
That willow done bowed down its head
asking to see some loving.

                    LILA
And I bet you done give it a show.

SUNSET

That ain't how Sunset falls. Every girl
got a spot. Some are pretty like a
twilight boat floating down the James
river. Some are dangerous like a back
porch or her husband's car. Sunset's
always searching for the spot. Sometimes
I find the girl first, another time the
place. When I get them both together then
we got us a good time. This willow spot,
this is magical. It's made by God out
here in the wilderness. A man and woman
get in a spot like that then something's
gonna come down on them.

LILA

You talk more foolishness than them fish
hands down to the docks. I'm spozed to
believe you got a magic wand under them
shorts and go lay out in the grass like a
couple of dogs?

SUNSET

You already seen what's in these pants and
you spozed to think that a man been half
way round the world would know how to use
it. Now, if he found him a special place
where nobody know and he willing to risk
lynching for one turn with you then you
got to figure some special love about to
fall. Can't nobody never know but you and
him so the question on this hot summer
afternoon is, "Do you want loving worth
dying for?"

                    SUNSET (cont'd)
Me, I'm heading out in the woods a
quarter mile and relaxing under that cool
willow off to the left of the path about
forty feet. I'm gonna walk slow cause
that's how Sunset like to come. If 'fore
long, a pretty girl were to happen along
then we gon' make ourselves a secret. You
take care of yourself Delilah.
(Exit Sunset left. Lila watches his back.
Pause.)

                    BLACK

                    THE END

TONGER

by e. shockley
(c) 1997
All Rights Reserved

CHARACTERS

JUNIOR PROSSER: A handsome, muscular, thirty-seven-year-old man who carries a long pole with pinchers on the end designed for dredging oysters.

JUNIOR

One and all
Draw near, draw near;
I'll spin a tale
To fill your ear.
The Tonger's craft
I'll demonstrate
If you will bid
Your journey wait.

Contrary to what appearance might suggest,
I mean no harm to any child of God. Draw
near. Fear not. I am no more than what you
see. The sum of my possessions are these
less than resplendent raiment, a first
class tonger's pole and the skill to dredge
an oyster from its muddy home in the
sea.... You don't understand a word of my
meaning, do you?..

*(Tonger gestures for them to watch then
climbs up onto a wall and brandishes his
tonger as if scooping oysters from the
bay.)*

On every civil month that carries in its
heart an "R" you will find me bobbing on the
deck of a sloop, knees slack, plucking from
the ocean bottom dainty manna...lumps of
delight...Oysters!!!! The fruit of the sea.

JUNIOR(cont'd)

For I a tonger be and were it not for this current month's desperate lack I would now be plying my trade.

"Mensibus erratis vos ostrea manducatis."

Let me speak plainly for I must hold your ear if I am to survive till again the skipbacks sail and restore me to my vocation... Everywhere upon which shines a sun that once did warm the Greeks of old, in any month without an "R" within its name a man may not an oyster sow nor sell. Doctors have argued that this ancient rule was made to guard us against a danger from the deep but I have had no faith in men of medicine since Dr. Benjamin Rush, learned scholar and sometime friend to Negroes, was led by his science to conclude that the darkened color of my skin was the result of leprosy. Instead I believe along with all who hunt the periwinkle in its bed, that the months from May through August entire are when the creatures spawn and thus to Tong would in a season bring us all to nothing. Instead only I and my like are turned out of nature's favor until Big Thursday when two thousand sloops will cast off against their fate. Until then I am the forlorn creature here before you, separated from calamity by wit alone.

JUNIOR(cont'd)

Were I escaped from the brutal jaws of
Southern bondage I might appeal to the
Abolition Societies and re-tell my woeful
tale and stunning escape. I was born to a
master who taught me the tonger's trade
before the law of 1780 required every slave
child to be apprenticed for twenty eight
years then set free. My mistress taught me
letters so that I might the family Bible
read and hearing those sacred words upon my
lips convinced them that to hold my soul in
captivity was to sin against God. This is
why my speech is as it is and further why
these months fall so hard upon my
shoulders. I survive the summers on the
kindness of dear friends like James Prosser
who knows how to make an oyster do
everything except vote. He plans to open
his own Saloon and stand like a man within
his establishment. He's found a place on
Eighth Street near Market. And you will do
yourself a kindness to dine when he opens
his doors. Or Mr. Robert Bogle, together
say with me his name. Shout it loud and you
will be rewarded for your pains. Together
like sloopers when the boatswain spots
shore, we will shout Robert Bogle on my
command.

(He raises the tonging pole and shouts.)

                    JUNIOR(cont'd)
Robert Bogle!!! And for everywhere within
scope of our collected voices, he is
renowned as the greatest caterer. Why he
once refolded the napkins at a wedding
because the bride had been prior divorced
from another. The things the man knows
would boggle the mind and the luckless he
feeds from the banquet remains might people
commons and crowd the gate.

     "Reckless if joy or grief prevail
     Stern, multifarious Bogle, hail!"

Men like these and more besides have taken
trades long despised and relegated all to
slaves or those of other low station then
through their efforts transformed these
bits of shell and folded napkin into
industries the envy of every man jack fresh
from Europe.

     (Holds up oyster shell)

They have fed my body, mind and soul; and
if they can thrive without banks to loan
money or laws to fully protect their rights
then I can live through this long summer on
blind oyster stew until I'm called again to
crest the waves.

JUNIOR(cont'd)
"Oooooh! Don't tell them that you saw me
 Or I may lose my job.
And then the oyster wiped away a tear.

 I've served in 47 stews
 Since 12 o'clock today
 For I'm the only oyster working here."

Would anybody like to buy an oyster shell?

THE END

LAST CALL

[A PLAY IN MODERN VERSE]
by e. shockley

CHARACTERS

BARKEEP...Local pub owner in West Port, Ireland

BOOZER......Young local

OLD MAN...Vagabond

AT RISE: Boozer sits warming himself by the fire as Barkeep busies himself with nothings. Rain is falling cruelly on the roof. Enter Old Man.

               OLD MAN
It has been said that in a bar
a well spun tale might earn a man
a draught of ale.

               BARKEEP
Such has been the case
on rare but rare occasion.

               OLD MAN
I have no wealth, not even time
just withered wit stands twixt these
bones and Satan's pit.

               BOOZER
Let him tell a tale, Keep,
there's room here by the fire.

               OLD MAN
I thank you, Sir; may God's good graces
keep you safe and guard you well
throughout this life.

               BOOZER
Don't get too familiar,
a chuckle's what I'm after.

OLD MAN
Then that you'll have! Attend my word;
I'll spin a yarn but first, friend, ale
to lube me horn.

BOOZER
Draw the prune a portion
afore he dies from thirsting.

BARKEEP
Let the crow drink hops
and save yourself a copper.

OLD MAN
You'll never hear O'Leary cry
against a sip of any brew
his fist can grip.

BARKEEP
Here you trounce, go choke
with himself by the fire.

OLD MAN
Take this for tip, "It isn't wise
to offer slight until you measure
someone's might."

BARKEEP
Save your sauce, Sausage,
and watch you don't get booted.
    (Old man crosses to the hearth.)

                    OLD MAN
To you, kind sir, I raise this mug
and both my feet. Hip, hip for hops.
Hooray for peat!

                    BOOZER
Wait! Don't drink it dry yet. You first
must tell a story.

                    OLD MAN
You needn't fear. I'll tell a tale
as sure as night is black and still
and full with fright.
I'll paint a wind that howls like Lear
and doors that creak on rusty hinge.
Did someone speak?

                    BOOZER
No one's breathed a word, chum,
since first you started railing.

                    OLD MAN
I guess a man who's been as long
alone as I will scare a hare
and hear a cry.

                    BOOZER
Trust my word, there's no one
about on this foul night.

OLD MAN
'Tis true it is an awful sky
more black than pitch. A perfect night
for ghoul or witch.

BOOZER
Make your tale a fright then,
with bogs and bugs and ghosties.

OLD MAN
Of all the stories that there be
to spill beside a hearth, tis this
that is my pride.
Short wick the candle. Ahh, that's better
light to tell a truthful tale
of earth and hell.

BARKEEP
I'll have no blaspheming...
last call on the Guinness.

BOOZER
Draw me out a bucket and
give me friend a fresh pint.

OLD MAN
If conscience lived within me but a
trace, your kindness, Sir, might strike
my black soul blind.

BARKEEP
Do you want a swigger,
aye or nay? It's last call.

        BOOZER
Sure he wants a swallow.
Now go on with your yarning.

        OLD MAN
I'd love to weave a clever tale
but you deserve a chance at life,
so brace your nerve.
What next I tell is true complete.
It may sound mad but mark me close.
And prosper, Lad.
The Innkeep here is very like
the common lot I've met thus far,
but you are not.
Now look at me. Look close and heed
the evidence. Believe that Death will
follow me hence.

        BOOZER
Wonderful! A grand start.

        BARKEEP
Starts are rare as feathers;
every bird has got one.

        BOOZER
Don't give him satisfaction.

        OLD MAN
My fate has been to bear the slight
of every slack who has the breath
to launch attack.

BARKEEP
Keep pronouncing names
and see if age protects you.

BOOZER
Save your threats, ya walrus.
There's no one here to heed you.

BARKEEP
Nonetheless, I'll not
be made to eat his cabbage.

BOOZER
Just ignore his blather.
His soul is sour like cut lime.

OLD MAN
The crinkles that traverse this head
were earned each one. I've heard as bad
and much worse done.
This very night, in point of fact,
a man will lose his life unless
he marks the clues.

BARKEEP
Make the fart police his tongue!

BOOZER
Beard of Christ, Innkeeper!

BARKEEP
He tugs my mustache.

BOOZER
It's nothing but a story.

                    BARKEEP
I've no gut for tales
that stink of death and magic.

                    OLD MAN
Then mine I'm sure you will not like.

                    BOOZER
I paid for the porter.

                    BARKEEP
That I can't deny,
tis true as I'm a Christian.

                    BOOZER
So leave us peace to drink it.

                    OLD MAN
This time I'm sure I heard a sound.
Quick, bolt the door!

                    BOOZER
Middle night is long past.
There's not a fish about now.

                    BARKEEP
Then where'd he come from?

                    OLD MAN
A land more far away than is
the sky above a mole. Did you
see something move?

BOOZER
Rats in bars are nature; they keep the
cats from starving.

BARKEEP
"Who are you expecting?"
that's what you should ask him.

OLD MAN
And if I said, as true as tripe,
you'd not believe. I've tried before.
Come, we must leave.

BOOZER
Leave you say? Not likely.
This hearth's as warm as any.

OLD MAN
But many men have sat so long
they learned too late that hearths grow
cold. Let's not tempt fate.

BOOZER
Tell me, what's your name, sir?

OLD MAN
Most days my name is misery.

BOOZER
And nights? What are you called then?

OLD MAN
Most nights I'm best called scared; then
cold again at last.

BOOZER
Cold's a name that suits you
there huddled by the fire.
Now that you're all toasted,
I want to hear my story.

OLD MAN
I pay my debts and some besides;
but come, let's walk down near the bogs
and have our talk.

BARKEEP
Go and fare ye well;
I'll send your mum a flower.

OLD MAN
He's right, it's not the least bit wise.
The chance exists that I'm a rook
but take the risk.

BOOZER
Not that I'm afearing,
but here is where I'll stay, friend.

OLD MAN
I'll quickly tell my story then,
Although I ought to hurry hie
before I'm caught.

                    BARKEEP
Ha! I knew the law
had interest in your goings.

                    OLD MAN
It's not the law of man, I fear,
that follows me. I'll tell a tale
and you will see. It had its start as
many score of year ago as there be grains
of dust below this wooden floor.
You see, young man, though I look old I'm
more than that. When truth is told, not
tens are used to mark the leagues since
my first cry. I've found a way to never
die.

                    BARKEEP
God that's rich! I knew
the bird was bubbles first off.

                    BOOZER
Hush, why don't you! Go on.
This preface suits me nicely.

                    OLD MAN
Just look around. Don't turn your head!
The eyes alone should move. Listen!
Hear it? A moan?

                    BARKEEP
That's a cat in heat.
Don't let him tug your trousers.

                    OLD MAN
Perhaps it is a lonesome cat.
Before the sun returns we'll know,
but I must run.

                    BOOZER
Why not wait till morning?
At least it's dry and warm here.

                    OLD MAN
Were I to wait beyond this hour,
there is no doubt from in this place
I'd not leave out.

                    BARKEEP
I can guarantee
you'll exit 'fore the morning.

                    OLD MAN
The corner, Lad, but don't turn round.
Take half a glance on my word. Go!
You missed your chance.

                    BOOZER
Chance? What chance? You've lost me.
Is this part of your story?

                    OLD MAN
It's part and all, the start and end.

                    BARKEEP
Ho!

                    BOOZER
What?

                    BARKEEP
Behind the keg.

                    BOOZER
There's nothing here, Gov.

                    BARKEEP
I thought I saw a specter.

                    BOOZER
It's just a lantern shadow.

                    OLD MAN
Perhaps my song has touched his toe.
And rubbed it wrong.

                    BARKEEP
You, you leave my pub
and take your demons with you.

                    OLD MAN
I'll leave. In fact, quite glad I am
to face the rain since Death would win
should I remain.

                    BOOZER
Age makes Death seem nearer
but still to leave is madness.

                    OLD MAN
It may seem queer but trust me, Lad,
the weather's bite is naught against
who's here tonight. I'm sure by now that
you must feel the brilly breath of man's
last friend upon this earth.

                    BOOZER
Add a brick of peat, Mate;
the chill will soon go running.

                    OLD MAN
I'm sure you're sure, as sure you should
assume I'm struck by moonstroke; still,
why press your luck? Perhaps I'm daft,
then you'll be wet and none the worse
come morrow morn. And yet, a hearse will
be your home if there's a bone in what I
claim. Mark me close, son; on God's great
name I swear to you that I have dodged
the Reaper's blade for seven score. My
debt's been paid, no, overpaid by fellows
standing in the wake. Death misses me
then stoops to take whomever's left
behind.

                    BOOZER
Christ, if that were so, Sir,
then you'd be quite the monster.

                    OLD MAN *(Starting to exit)*
Perhaps. I cannot say. I value life
enough to pay this awful price.

                    BARKEEP
Eh, now, you can't dash,
not with the heavens bawlin'.

                    OLD MAN
My welcome's worn just like these shoes.

                    BARKEEP
I'm the one to tell ya
when your visit's grown stale.

                    OLD MAN
Sir Conan Doyle could read these clues
without his glass. You've said as much
and more in fact, so what's the point
in this new tact?

                    BARKEEP
Can't a fella change his tune
without explaining?

                    BOOZER
Still it is peculiar
to see you turned about so.

                    BARKEEP
Let it be peculiar
long as Grandpa stays put.

                    OLD MAN
The type of mind that looks for guile
could find its share in this attempt
to keep me here.

                    BARKEEP
I don't care a flea
for what you find, you're staying.

          (Barkeep places a gun on the bar.)

                    BOOZER
Have you shed your senses?

                    BARKEEP
I'm as clear as water
from a tap in Sligo.

                    BOOZER
Just put away the pistol.

                    BARKEEP
Have you heard one bit
of what this man's been saying?
Once he leaves this tavern
one of us will pass on.

                    BOOZER
Man, have you been nipping?

                    BARKEEP
Don't you see the demons
dancing in the shadows?

                    BOOZER
I see you've lost your pebbles.

            OLD MAN
He thinks he can detain me here
until the thresh will take my soul
and leave this flesh as food for flies.
A murderer he is as sure as goats are
gaunt when grazing's poor.

            BARKEEP
There you've got the kettle
railing 'gainst a skillet.
Care to count the times
you've left and Death came creeping?

            BOOZER
If you know what's best, chum,
you'll give himself the humor.

            BARKEEP
When the cock cries day
God bless and fare thee well, Sir.

            OLD MAN
I'm not a man who can be told
to stay as like he were a dog.

            BOOZER
Why provoke his lordship?
Let's pass the night in comfort.

            OLD MAN
If just for spite and nothing more, I'll
risk the spittle from his gun. It's you
and I, God's will be done. For sure as

                    OLD MAN (cont'd.)
sheep need shearing or a cow a squeeze,
I'd sooner die than scrape my knees to
bow before the like of you.

                    BARKEEP
Let your pride run rowdy
and find out where you end.

                    OLD MAN
I'll fill a hole the same as you, sir,
damn your soul.

                    BOOZER
You should stop and think, please,
before you both are sorry.

                    OLD MAN
I've carried grief within this breast
for many scores. I've broken hearts and
stood where wars have made the earth a
muddy swamp of bloody bone. I've left a
hearth to walk alone through brittle
rain, abandoned disbelieving maids when
dawn had yet to paint their beds...
The cards I've played to snooker Death
may well have lost my only soul but from
the post past pillar pole, through grin
and tear, I've never yet, despite it all,
known true regret.

                    BARKEEP
That's because your heart's
as hard as winter farmland.

                    OLD MAN
I've done my share of dirty deeds
but with this act you've passed my all
and that's a fact.

                    BARKEEP
All I've done is saved
my rump from getting roasted.

                    OLD MAN
You've done that much but more as well.
You've cut me short the same as if you'd
slit my throat.

                    BARKEEP
You'd have served as like
a turn to me I'd wager.

                    OLD MAN
Your money you would lose as sure as
Gypsies dance.

                    BARKEEP
That we'll never know
because I've got you sighted.

                    BOOZER
Easy now, McGreggor;
you mustn't crowd the trigger.

                    OLD MAN
Say what you like; you had the chance to
go with me, or on your own to confront

                    OLD MAN *(cont'd.)*
this thing because I chose to sit
and sing instead of creeping in and out
before you learned my shadow's name and
both were burned.

                    BARKEEP
Tell it to Saint Peter
when you get to heaven.

                    BOOZER
Come tomorrow morning
we'll sip our tea and chuckle
neigh till half past noontime
remembering this madness.

                    OLD MAN
I'll have my laugh tonight or
not at all.

                    BARKEEP
I vote not at all.

                    OLD MAN
You're quick to think I've turned
my final trick.

                    BARKEEP
My gun is cocked and loaded.
Test your luck if you've a mind
but woe upon you.

OLD MAN
A man could not have lived as long as I
without a score of way for giving rout to
weasels, crows and applegates.

BARKEEP
Take your shot then take a shot
and see who God loves.

BOOZER
Wait, you two!

OLD MAN
No need to fret.

BOOZER
I've often from less a cause
seen blood spilled.

OLD MAN
That may well be, but I am yet to meet
the man who owns a heart could call my
dare and rest assured the man's not here.

BARKEEP
You can grieve your mother come the
morning or now.

OLD MAN
And you can greet the gallows, chum,
when next they swing.

                    BARKEEP
Gallows?

                    OLD MAN
Don't fear, my friend. It will not sting.

                    BARKEEP
I've no business with the hangman, thank
you.

                    OLD MAN
You don't believe they give awards
for gunning down old travelers?
Well, do you now?

                    BARKEEP
When I tell the truth of it....

                    OLD MAN
"Your lordship, let me please explain.
I sent his soul to meet the Lord
because a ghoul was set to pounce....

                    BARKEEP
Alright.

                    OLD MAN
"...the instant that he left my pub, I
had no choice..."

                    BARKEEP
Enough now! Though it's nearly worth the
price to end your foul works.

OLD MAN
Always a rub. Perhaps I'm just a barfly
who has learned the trade of making tales
to swap for mead.

BOOZER
Sure as sure you've well earned
your fill of stout this evening.

OLD MAN
If I were half of what you say then you'd
agree to leave this Inn along with me.
The both of you in fact could flee into
the rain. We might survive to meet again
and baffle Death who can collect but one
poor bloke on each foray.

BOOZER
If your tale were Gospel I'd still not
leave this tavern.

OLD MAN
I'd say you spoke more like a fool
than as a lad with all of life open ahead
like a new wife.

BOOZER
Life is in this tavern as sure as
anywhere else.

OLD MAN
But Death is right behind your chair...

                    BOOZER
There is where he's been since
the midwife smacked my bottom.

                    OLD MAN
...just standing there with coal for eyes
and fire red hair, his scythe as sharp as
clever Hans the counting horse. If you
saw, you'd see it's far worse than facing
rain, or cold or night or any plum from
Nature's purse.

                    BARKEEP
Get your things and leave, Tom.
This is more than blather.

                    BOOZER
Then, my friend, how is it
that you've not packed a duffle?

                    BARKEEP
I've poured out my blood
with every pint of Guinness.
This old pub is all
that makes the bitters go down.

                    OLD MAN
I know you're dumb, but don't believe
you mean to say a pile of brick
is worth your life.

                    BARKEEP
Such a man as you would see a heap of
worn stone. You who have no hook
to hang your mothworn hat on. Me, despite
complaining 'bout the price of barley,
I know every precious bit of worth
to my life comes from pouring cheer and
wringing smiles from faces that might
otherwise have frozen fast and fearsome.

                    OLD MAN
We each must pick a load to bear. You've
told me yours and I've shared mine. You
choose to stay and that is fine enough by
me. In fact, I'm glad that you were here
to fill my cup with lukewarm beer and
offer shelter from the cold.

                    BARKEEP
Save your sour breath for had I had one
small clue I'd have bolted door and
window fast against you.

                    OLD MAN
Then we are both, it seems, cut from a
single cloth.

                    BARKEEP
Take the Kid and go before the fire burns
out.

              BOOZER
If you haven't noticed, I'm wearing
proper trousers.

              OLD MAN
The long pants cannot hide your youth.
You've walked this land too little to
understand, Lad, the mysteries and
many dangers of this earth.

              BOOZER
Soon enough I'll know them.

              OLD MAN
But soon's too late much like the moth
who learns his folly once a wing ignites
in flame.

              BARKEEP
Hurry man, the morning glare is rising
quickly.

              BOOZER
Just leave if you've a mind to go.

              OLD MAN
I'll do just that and bare no blame for
what may follow in my wake.

              BOOZER
Any fate is surely a better lot than your
life.

                    BARKEEP
Pack your gear and shut the door behind
you. Bar's closed.

                    BOOZER
You will have to pitch me and be
forewarned I'm no slouch.

                    BARKEEP
If I must I'll do my best and devil take
the loser.

                    OLD MAN
Just humor me one final time and try to
see the hungry beast that's perched there
on the window seat.

                    BOOZER
I can see him clear as the waters of the
Liffey; teeth and scythe and black eyes,
the slender sharp clawed fingers...

                    BARKEEP
If you see the bugger well then why won't
you run?

                    BOOZER
No man born save Jesus can hope to dodge
the Reaper.

                    OLD MAN
Of course we face a sure defeat but
sooner late than now I say. Let's run him
cross the sluice and back.

                    BOOZER
Is it worth the bother?

                    OLD MAN
We clean the moss from round our barns
despite the fact that, sure as damp will
follow fog, we'll light a lamp and find a
clump of green in just the place where
last we scrubbed.

                    BOOZER
But if each day from night to bright
all I did was scrape moss then hustle
t'ward the next green barn, not a soul to
call a friend, in point of fact, no one
alive, far as I know, in any room whose
door has slapped my butt, I confess I'm
hard pressed to call that fate a proper
life.

                    OLD MAN
The world, my boy, is vast. Most any
life's a proper life, if you're alive. I
pay a price and I survive the same as you
or he.

                    BARKEEP
No, it's not the same.

                    OLD MAN
Says who?

                    BOOZER
Every inch of you screams it.

                    BARKEEP
You're lonely as an old sock.

                    OLD MAN
And do you think the both of you don't
wear the stink of wasted lives the same
as me?

                    BOOZER
Not the same nor nearso.

                    OLD MAN
You're right. It's worse by twelves! At
least I don't rehearse my death. I run
and duck and dodge and snatch at each
reprieve. I stand upon the breach and
earn the daily thrill of leaping back a
pace to laugh in Death's green frowning
face.

                    BOOZER
Death laughs right back at you.
you've missed near every pleasure.

                    BARKEEP
Have you had one single friend in all
your decades?

                    OLD MAN
Come join me, lad. I'll tell him, "Yes!
I have a chum!" Don't let the Reaper
strike you dumb.

                    BOOZER
Dumb I may well be, sir, but only fools
run from life.

                    OLD MAN
I wish that I had half a day to sway you
from your narrow view.

                    BOOZER
Don't lose sleep about me and I'll not
curse nor cry for you.

                    OLD MAN
The dawn is come. I'll lay a rose upon
your grave and pull a weed. We'll know in
time who's right. God's speed.

          (*Exit Old man*)

                    BARKEEP
May the Devil claim your soul and feed
you brimstone! Damn you! Damn you twice
again!... Maybe it's a lie. Sure, the
drink and dark and damp and talk of dry
bones made me think I saw a wolf in every
shadow.

          (*Barkeep tries the "seeing
          exercise."*)

                    BARKEEP (cont'd.)
No one's here but you and I and several
rodents. Come on, Lad; let's down a stout
then grab a few snores. Bring your glass
on over to the tap, it's my treat...

       BARKEEP (cont'd.)
Have you set to dozing in my fav'rite
armchair?... Don't play games 'cause
I'm not in a merry humor.

    *(Barkeep touches Boozer. A cock
    crows.)*

BLACK

SECTION FIVE

THE REIMAGINED
THEATRE

*"If you could see
What I see
As I see it,
You would know
What I know
That I know."*
journal entry 4/21/93

*"Ignorance is the shortest distance
between two mistakes."
journal entry 9/13/94*

THE OEDIPUS CONSPIRACY

The conceptualization of art as a pure aesthetic is a recent phenomenon and wholly false. Subjectivity dominates the selection process of every epoch. One convincing demonstration of this reality rests in an exposé of the documented sociopolitical machinations that underpin the selection of Sophocles as the model of Greek—and thereafter European—theatrical perfection.

The number of theatrical victories attributed to the work of Sophocles[72] far exceed those of his closest rivals Aeschylus and Euripides. His masterwork, *Oedipus Rex*, selected by Aristotle as the model for *The Poetics*, has been commonly accepted as defining both Hellenistic drama

---

[72] Best known for his plays *Antigone, Oedipus Rex* and *Electra*, this Greek tragedian set standards and aesthetics for theatre that are followed to this day. Aeschylus won thirteen first place victories and Euripides won five. Sophocles, however won twenty four and never placed less than second whenever he entered the competiton.

and dramaturgical excellence for more than two thousand years. An examination of the life of Sophocles reveals that political factors were more significant than aesthetic values in identifying his plays as worthy of singular praise.

Sophocles was born in 497 B.C. His father, Sophilus, was purported to have been a munitions manufacturer. Such an important role in Greek life placed the family squarely among the Athenian ruling class. Sophocles, in fact, was considered especially blessed. He led the victorious dance following the pivotal Greek triumph at Salamis. He enjoyed a long career as public servant, was respected as a general and entombed in Athens after an enviable and distinguished life.

Only two scandals endure to haunt his name. One is the possibility of significant military defeat at the hands of Melissus in the Samian war. The other is a historic charge of impropriety during the judging of his first victorious trilogy. The latter event is of enormous relevance to any study of the impact of politics upon theatre history.

It is well documented that an elaborate and seemingly incorruptible system existed for adjudicating the major festivals of Hellenistic Greece. Ten judges were chosen by lots to represent each of the prominent gens (clans). After watching the program of trilogies, followed by satyr plays, each judge wrote a ballot. Three of these were drawn from an urn and the other seven burned.

This system had been in place for several decades when Sophocles arrived fresh from the events at Salamis with his first offering, *Tryptolemus*, in tow. In that same year, the time honored selection process was abandoned and a tribunal of generals was appointed to decide the laurel wreath recipient.

Being the son of a munitions manufacturer, Sophocles very likely would have enjoyed some small advantage in this context. The possibility for favoritism increased since the favored son had recently been awarded a significant military honor by these same general/judges. Still, other authors may have won similar or even superior martial acclaim, which might suggest that the agreement was simply to award the coveted prize to some veteran rather than a conspiracy to champion Sophocles.

Regardless of the motives, it is certain that General Cimon was one of the adjudicators. He was also an acknowledged friend of Sophocles and a member of "The Company of the Educated[73]," a group founded by Sophocles to ponder the pertinent questions of the day. Thus, even if General Cimon was truly incorruptible, he still had been influenced by and was an influence on the young author. Their lifelong collaboration suggests that they shared an outlook or aesthetic that would predispose the General to select *Tryptolemus* for honors.

Unfortunately, no copy of the play exists; but that is irrelevant within the context of this argument. The seven surviving complete manuscripts and various fragments of his other work affirm the literary abilities of Sophocles. *Tryptolemus* would have been easy to select

---

[73] There is a detailed account of this relationship in *Introduction To Sophocles* (see bibliography).

as the superior work in a subjective environment where competitors were more likely "different from" than "superior to" one another.

A comparison of the ultimate fates of the three acknowledged greatest Greek tragedians reinforces the assertion that sociopolitical agendas may have influenced the victory of Sophocles. Aeschylus and Euripides both faced government censure and chose to pass their later lives on foreign soil. Sophocles lived his entire life as an honored Athenian and then was remembered by comic poet Phrynichus as...

> "...*a man fortunate and successful, who made many fine tragedies. And finely did he die, having had no evil to endure...*"

The possible motive for a government or a military enclave within Athenian society to select Sophocles as its major propagandist is not difficult to identify. Both Aeschylus and Euripides had been influenced by the treasonous teachings of Anaxagoras. An apostle of Zarathustra, he had an enormously disruptive impact upon the state as the phenomenon of a bloodless coup—the foundation of Persian imperialism—threatened to topple the Greek army.

The list of exiles and executions associated with that religious expansionism was enormous. Anaxagoras was threatened with death but rescued by the intervention of Pericles. Aspasia, second wife of Pericles, was of

Melesian birth and charged with impiety in an attempt to disrupt a powerful Zarathustrian cell that included Themistocles, Diogenes, Archelaus, Damonides, Socrates, Euripides and, at least tangentially, Aeschylus.

A reconstruction of Zarathustrian philosophy and the campaign of apostolic expansion requires an entire paper of its own. The relevant detail here is that several nations had been undone from within by the concept of God as a transcendent reality. (The ultimate Christian revolution that culminated in the alleged conversion of Roman Emperor Constantine closely resembles the Hellenistic Greek fear of Persian philosophy.) The climate created a desperate need for a propagandist committed to traditional Hellenistic ideals.

Aeschylus was a candidate for this office. His military background had indoctrinated him in the ideology of "strict law." Deeds are ends; punishments follow upon them without consideration of explanatory motives. Had he remained true to this credo, perhaps he might have co-existed with Sophocles, but the older dramatist proved willing also to champion the individual. The clear evidence of this philosophical shift is present in his play, *The Eumenides*, which concludes with a successful defense of Orestes' matricide based upon an examination of the motivations for his accursed behavior.

The other great tragedian, Euripides, was certainly the rival of Sophocles in talent but his radical politics and close associations with Anaxagoras marked his as thoroughly unacceptable to state propagandists. He openly championed the individual and ignored or devalued the omnipotence of Gods. Medea, for example, enacts her revenge without recourse to Prophesy, then escapes through supra-human, but not divine, intervention.

Both outcast authors, despite a separation of age, class and station, appear similarly unacceptable as propagandists. Sophocles, by contrast, is well suited to the task. His works are a harkening back to pre-Hellenistic origins. He affirms the inescapability of the Gods' decrees, the infallibility of oracles, and he canonizes heroic figures from the mythic past.

Sophocles continued on from his first victory with *Tryptolemus* to quill many laurelled trilogies. The Oedipal story, his best known surviving creation, became the standard for dramatic structure for millennia. This work, therefore, should contain in its plot and symbols the philosophies that affirm the class of the author's champions.

I. THE SYMBOLS IN SOPHOCLES

Oedipus is set in Thebes, a Greek city and successor to the earlier Egyptian city of the same name. Thus begins a series of Sophoclean references that reaffirm the traditional Hellenistic ruling class religion.

The Egyptian Thebes [hereafter identified as "old Thebes"] was purported to be home of the Oedipus Cult which performed a winter ritual that involved symbolic death and rebirth as a corollary to the changing of the seasons.

Various mythologies identify Agenor as the figure who introduced this worship into Theban culture. Agenor was also commonly known as father of Kadmos (or Cadmos). Kadmos [whose name may come from "Queddem" or "easterner"] was mythic founder of Thebes and grandfather to Oedipus.

The Sphinx is another clear pre-Hellenistic reference in Sophocles' most famous play. The most famous is the monument to Horus at Giza. Numerous accounts identify Apollo as the Hellenized transmutation of Horus. This identifies the Sophoclean masterwork as an affirmation of the ancient sun cult centered in Horus/Apollo.

These discoveries are useful both to more effectively interpret the play, *Oedipus,* and to identify the philosophies being advanced by the Greek military enclave (which may have been in opposition to the oligarchy or the state). The Sphinx of Egypt and of Sophocles, as well as the Greek God Apollo, are each associated with riddle. The entire plot of the play rests upon the successful unraveling of various oracular declarations and especially the riddle of the Sphinx.

```
"What walks on four legs in the
morning, two at noon, and on
three legs in the evening?"
```

Oedipus answers, "Man," whereupon the Sphinx destroys itself and he is awarded his widowed mother as bride.

The death of the Sphinx/Sun God and its resurrection in the form of confirmed prophecy is entirely in keeping with the winter cult origins of Oedipus worship. The Horus/Apollo correlation, however, introduces entirely new perspectives. Several sun worship cults utilize the same riddle but with a different answer. It is the sun itself that crawls in the morning, stands tall at noontime, then hobbles off at night. Oedipus is now guilty of misinterpreting the oracle, dooming his people and committing atrocities.

Sophocles was undoubtedly aware of the intricate interpretations of sun mythology. He enjoyed a close friendship with Herodotus, the foremost Greek authority on Egyptian culture of his time. Furthermore, Sophocles himself was a priest of such renown in the Egyptian cult of Aesclepius that the altar was maintained in his house until the Athenian temple was completed.

Sophoclean dramatic choices clearly coincide with the sociopolitical philosophies of military traditionalists. The wise layman Oedipus proves himself desperately incompetent to analyze the Gods therefore he/we are wisest to obey unquestioningly. The affirmation of the inscrutability of oracles, as well as their infallibility, empowers whoever controls the priesthood.

This knowledge of Egyptian Sphinx lore and Sun worship calls for a reexamination of the structure in the writing of Sophocles. The entire play, *Oedipus Rex*, may well be a riddle. The title character frequently speaks passages composed almost exclusively of questions. These could be interpreted as establishing a pattern wherein he speaks truth as inquiries and falsehood as statements.

"Come now, tell me, where have
you proved yourself a seer?"

[*True. Teiresius has not proven himself a seer yet.*]

"Why, when the watcher was here
who wove dark song, did you say
nothing that could free this
folk?"

[*True. He did not speak and deliver the people.*]

"Yet the riddle, at least, was
not for the first comer to read."

[*False. "Fear the Gods and submit," was plain from the first.*]

"There was need of a seer's
skill, and none such were you
found to have either by help of
birds or as known from any God."

[*False. A seer was not needed since Oedipus is none.
Also, the skill of Teiresius is later proven true.*]

"No, I came, I Oedipus the
ignorant, and made her mute when
I had seized the answer by my
wit..."

[*False. She is not mute, he has an incorrect answer.*]

"And it is I whom you are trying
to oust, thinking to stand close
to Creon's throne."

[*False. Teiresius has no concern for Creon and the throne.*]

This pattern can be applied throughout the play. If, on occasion, it is inconsistent, then one must ask if it is the concept or the translation that is at fault. Also, if Sophocles did develop an oracular approach to language in this text, then it may reveal new interpretations of other characters. Is Creon subject to the same rules when he asks, "How then could royalty be sweeter for me than painless rule and influence?" Certainly he appears to enjoy royalty immensely in later plays. One also might inquire if this pattern continues for Oedipus throughout the play or does he reconcile speech and idea after blinding himself? Is he truly "hateful to the Gods" or has the transformation of status that is completed at Colonus already begun?

Again, further exploration of this particular feature in Sophoclean writing stands outside the purposes of this paper. What is germane is the observation that the play structure can be interpreted as additional evidence of devotion to the religious traditions of the Oedipal and Sphinx cults. In other words, "that old time religion."

II. ALTERATIONS OF TRADITIONAL MYTHOLOGY

The same mythology was the source of most Hellenistic drama. Sophocles is certainly not unique in his use of Egyptian references. The alterations that he makes in these commonly known stories, however, reveal his personal philosophies and political leanings.

One clear example of Sophoclean myth tinkering is the removal of culpability from the history of Oedipus.

Tradition had accredited Laius with the rape and murder of Chrysippus, son of Pelops. The story was used to explain the origins of pederasty. There is at least one version of this same story suggesting that the fatal battle between father and son was not the result of roadside improprieties but rather the conclusion of a homosexual jealousy.

There are dramatic arguments for both the original myths and the Sophoclean simplification. Either story could be theatrically exciting. The political agenda of inspiring blind obedience, however, is most effectively championed by a blameless Oedipus. In the world of Sophocles, this fine young man is guilty only of hubris. Such positioning exalts the power of the Gods.

Repeatedly, Sophocles structures his plays to exploit what Moses Hadas calls "the traditional level of heroic remoteness." By that he means the alterations or versions of myth that Sophocles selects serve to celebrate the heroic or messianic qualities of Greek icons.

Euripides' *Medea* is a wildly passionate woman who knowingly uses a poisoned garment to destroy her rival; in Sophocles' *Trachinian Women*, Deianeira also uses a poisoned garment but with the thought that the drug is beneficent, not lethal.

Those aesthetic and thematic choices inspired the ruling military class of Athens to embrace their gifted author. His considerable dramatic skill was wholly devoted to celebrating traditional Greek religious and cultural ideals. It can be argued, therefore, that his plays were preferred by judges of religious festivals sponsored by state appointed patrons.

CONCLUSION

The times demanded that traditional values be reiterated. A plague had preceded the Peloponnesian Wars. Zarathustrianism and its derivative, Sophism, threatened a mass conversion of Athenian citizenry. Greek civilization was under cultural assault.

Sophocles possessed the requisite literary ability, religious orthodoxy and Hellenistic jingoism to be chosen by General Cimon among others to lead the philosphical defense of the nation. Viewing Western drama's preeminent figure in this political context demonstrates that the evolution of theatre arts is a sociopolitical phenomenon. The merits of Sophocles the author were far less significant than his usefulness as a propagandist in defining his place in history.

"It's not who you know, it's not what you know; it's who you know who likes you."

Robert Maurice Riley

***

*"They say the cream rises to the top but it
may just be that fat floats."
journal entry 2/4/93*

PRACTICAL APPLICATIONS OF
MULTICULTURALISM

(A REPORT ON THE "PHILADELPHIA VOICE IN
DRAMA CONFERENCE.")

Contemporary American society is undergoing an intellectual revolution. There is a call for a revision of history that acknowledges the contributions of diverse cultures and more accurately reflects both genders. Most people will readily concede the moral preference of multiculturalism; but unless some creative imperative accompanies the new mandate, then it will only be another politically correct albatross around the necks of playwrights who behind closed doors believe that Aristotle defines the poetics of theatre.

On November 26, 1994, at 10:10 a.m. in the Tomlinson Theatre on the campus of Philadelphia's Temple University, an audience of sixty authors assembled to explore the question, "What would happen to our work if we were to radically reimagine theatre history?" The event was the inaugural panel of a day-long conference sponsored jointly by the Philadelphia Dramatists' Center (PDC) and the Temple Playwrights' Center.

Seated onstage were Michael Hollinger (Haas Award winner and resident writer for the Arden Theater), Sydne Mahone (literary manager for Crossroads Theatre and editor/contributor of *Moon Marked and Touched By The Sun: Plays of African American Women)*, Rosanna Yamagiwa Alfaro (author of the East/West Players hit, *Mishima)* and myself as moderator.

Each participant had been instructed to prepare an extreme position statement that presented a particular culture, nation or ethnicity so that it occupied the place of highest relevance in the history and practice of theatre. This exercise was then to be followed by an open discussion wherein the diverse theatrical philosophies would hopefully be combined into some larger aesthetic that more effectively represented the global community.

Eurocentric, Womanist, Afrocentric, and Asian-Pacific American viewpoints were chosen because of their diversity and their familiarity to the panelists. It was conceded from the first that the act of selecting presupposes some process of editing and therefore bias. This unidentified and largely happenstance bias would ultimately affect the result when the attempt was made to recombine the four extremist positions into some new inclusive model for theatre history and poetics.

Michael Hollinger was selected to speak first. His task was to summarize and defend the status quo. Toward this end he offered, tongue in cheek, a sequential outline. It began with the glorious Greeks and progressed successively through robust Romans, marvelous Medieval Mysteries, then elegant Elizabethan experiments in theatre. These were followed by the "well-made play" movement as represented by Henrik Ibsen and finally an amorphous "modern drama" that remains dominated by Aristotelian conceptions of catharsis and theme.

He eloquently argued the extreme platform that every significant refinement in theatre history was the product of Anglo-Saxon ingenuity and as he spoke, his words sounded frighteningly similar to the prefaces of many university textbooks. Throughout his presentation the contributions of other cultures were routinely appropriated or ignored. Specific examples included references to Terence Afer without acknowledging his African heritage and mention of Brecht *sans* the anonymous Chinese texts that inspired works like *The Caucasian Chalk Circle*.

It also became clear that this linear perspective on history confined itself exclusively to a single class of European society. It was the history of kings and their entertainments. The peasant and folk arts that existed concurrent with the royal theatres were systematically ignored.

As she championed a Womanist history, Sydne Mahone identified many of these omissions. She chose to use the advice that her mother and aunts had given her regarding the rearing of children as the foundation for formulating rules of drama. In her aesthetic, the audience or society was substituted for the toddler and the text was the communicator of maternal edict.

Catharsis was not among the instructions that Ms. Mahone received in parenting therefore it was not central to the new aesthetic. "Pity and fear" likewise were omitted. No longer was a single thesis the intended result of a two-hour discourse. The new goals were to nurture, to instill an unwavering belief in a constant love, to teach sharing, to comfort and then ultimately to empower.

In order to achieve its stated goals, this Womanist theatre might embrace pageant or storytelling forms. It might present a pastiche of moments alternately danced, sung, enacted, etc., and let its audience select which sections they will invest with meaning. The modern proscenium might be assessed as antithetical to the concept of nurturing since it separates performer from audience. Broadway might be displaced by PS122 as the apex of contemporary theatre.

The act of placing the mother at the center of the paradigm flies in the face of the historic European theatrical tradition of chauvinism. Entire generations of women have been banned from the audience and stage of Aristotelian-inspired theatres and so it is logical that their thinking has been unwelcome in the formulation of aesthetic principals.

It was noted that despite the obstacles to inclusion, women have impacted greatly on the Eurocentric theatre and suffer the same process of intellectual appropriation as Brecht's Chinese collaborators. An example is Hrotsvitha of Gandersheim (circa 935-73) who is noted for her Terence-inspired liturgical plays that contributed to formulating the Medieval Mystery play movement. Ntozake Shange's *For Colored Girls Who Have Considered Suicide When The Rainbow Is Enough* is another example. It enjoyed commercial success while mooning the rules of Aristotle's ancient poetics and gave inspiration to the performance artists who now routinely explore rule-breaking in alternative theatres across America.

Finally, Ms. Alfaro presented her thoughts in a short paper but began by admitting the difficulty that she had encountered in her attempts to re-see her culture in a position of preeminence. Japanese-Americans have been so traditionally marginalized in American theatre that she was in effect being asked to restructure everything from the proscenium through to Stanislavski's ideas of good acting.

Her response was to utilize personal narrative to poke fun at cultural bias in literature. She explained that her husband is Colombian. Is her daughter, a painter, therefore expected to create Japanese-Colombian works with airbrushes? Culture is a hodgepodge of intermarriage, invasion, trade and often unadulterated admiration. She conceded that there are shared cultural experiences that collectively influence generations of authors (such as the Japanese-American internees during World War II), but the idea of attributing creation of theatre, or a theatrical style, to a single segment of any one society is ludicrous.

It was demonstrated that every author is simultaneously a member of several cultures. Common bonds are shared among immigrants, parents, political parties, religions, regions of the country, professions, etc. Sensitivity to the diversity that exists within oneself allows one to write expansively as in the case of Ms. Alfaro. She has penned *Mishima*, a play about the revered Japanese author. She also has written *Baranacas*, which explores political strife in a fictitious Central American nation. *Pablo And Cleo* examines pathos in the life of Picasso and seems completely apropos for the mother of a painter.

There was a general acceptance of Ms. Alfaro's point. The assemblage seemed most eager to admit the need for a broadening of perspective in contemporary theatre and the popularity of her creations was applauded. Several authors confided, however, that they felt intimidated when writing outside of a comfort zone that was ultimately identified as white, male, Judeo-Christian characters in narrative plays.

The audience and panelists alike volunteered suggestions but I saw my function as the moderator to steer the discussion away from specifics and back to the larger question of whether reimagining theatre history—incorporating gender, class and cultural diversity—is a boon or a burden to theatre practitioners? It was at this moment that I uttered the words that every author had been waiting to hear. "Reimagining the origins and history of theatre should be embraced because it makes us better authors." Ultimately this is the only relevant issue to practicing writers.

Firstly, a directorial example was cited. Knowledge of Egyptian influences both in the life of Sophocles and evident throughout the text of *Oedipus Rex* inform interpretations of the language and themes. Sophocles was a priest in the Egyptian cult of Aesclepius. The riddle of the Sphinx is a prominent feature in the plot of the play. This and other evidence suggest that the entire work might be conceived as one huge riddle.

In a similar manner, interpretations of the works of Aeschylus and Euripides might be influenced by their having a knowledge of Persian culture. As I pointed out in the previous chapter, both authors were close acquaintances of Anaxagoras, a disciple of Zoroaster. Both authors were exiled from their homeland. Both had chosen to offer sympathetic portraits of foreigners in their works.

More contemporary examples would include Thornton Wilder's *Our Town*. Staging might be revised after studying his trip to China and the theatrical styles that he encountered there. Or knowledge of the history of Henri Christophe, first emperor of Haiti, and his relevance to *Emperor Jones* could inspire a dynamic reinterpretation of O'Neill's play.

Secondly, the changing demographics of the nation were cited. Currently the overwhelming majority of characters on the boards are white males. Broadening the cultural, ethnic and gender choices in one's work promises to invite a more representative (and therefore larger) audience into the theatre. The reimagined theatre speaks potentially to the global community more so than to a single locale.

Thirdly, the example of *Othello* was offered. Obviously the influence of Moorish culture impacts greatly upon the text. Also, however, that play stands out in the canon of Shakespeare's work for its uniqueness. Students might read it more readily than yet another history play about a guy named Henry.

Finally, reimagining offers challenges to an author. Obstacles, or more accurately the overcoming of them, are what reveal greatness. The impact of reimagining upon structure, character, subtext, theme or dialogue is so full of potential that it becomes veritably irresistible once it is understood.

A writer who does not embrace
the full cultural diversity of the world
has less clay from which to create.
***

"The face in the mirror remains continually mine."
journal entry 12/16/93

IT'S ALL MUSIC

One-half dozen box office records, numerous national and local awards, inclusion in the Lincoln Center Library, lunch with Kurt Vonnegut and John Guare, nearly one quarter of a century laboring in the American Musical Theatre can be reduced to three words: "It's all music."

I'm the guy who sits on the piano bench beside a Grammy award-winning composer selecting melodies to lyricize for the climatic close of an urban opera. I'm the quiet fella in the far corner of a rehearsal room whispering instructions to the stage manager before a nervous singer is asked to reinterpret an audition piece. I'm the red-eyed recluse living on coffee and Ding Dongs at two a.m. in the third week of rehearsal with a new finale due at breakfast.

The critics, the audiences and the calendar all are unforgiving. Their sole concern is that the event for which they have assembled and are sometimes paid be memorable. The voice mustn't crack on "G" over high "C." There must be a collective gasp when the young star faces his armed nemesis. The strains of some melody should nip at the edges of consciousness on the car ride home and in days to come. In a span of less than two hours, using melody, lyric and motion, I am required to somehow transform the lives of a room full of strangers.

These unequivocal demands sever all alliances to genre in the artists whose task it is to create this expectedly mesmerizing experience. I grew up on Motown but pen everything from bebop through Bartok in a desperate effort to infuse each instant of my penned moment on the boards with electricity.

Popular culture divides music. Press the seek button on a car radio; each stop along the frequency band carries a name and narrow play list: country, pop, rap, jazz, easy listening, R & B, classical, opera, plus an even longer list of subdivisions within each fictitious genre. Working, however, in an art form in which the character that sings a song is subject to sudden and radical revision reveals the commonalties more so than the differences between musical styles.

> *"There are only two kinds of music, the kind that sounds good and everything else."*
> Edward "Duke" Ellington

Watching Bessie Smith's former pianist, Little Brother Montgomery, teach former Miles Davis music director

Bobby Irving the voicings that made the 20's roar, affirms the reality of the Duke's mantra. The same song sung in a different "pocket" has a whole new "schwing!" (If you have to ask, you'll never know.)

Early in my career, I tended bar at New York's Frank Silvera Writers' Workshop during the record-setting run of my musical, *A Nite in the Life of Bessie Smith*. Uptown blues pianist Ron Burton was replaced for three performances by piano bar great Emme Kemp, and the change in the sound was striking. Burton's "kick it till it goes" quality gave way to an expansively voiced, delicate bed of music upon which big-throated Ebony Jo-Ann stood and hollered.

The lesson of those fifty-five performances became the mantra that ultimately won for me several of America's major music theatre awards. The marriage of Kemp's style and Burton's bottom is the essence of an artistic challenge that spans millennia.

Dr. Brenda Dixon-Gottschild defines the two approaches to art as manifestations of European classicism and a West African aesthetic called Nommo.

The ancient Athenian Greeks expressed this same dualism in their worship of Dionysius and Apollo. It has been articulated as a "mind/body dichotomy," style versus content, macro/micro, east/west, melody/funk... It's all music.

The subtle quality of Nommo makes it elusive. The technical difficulty of the Classical or Apollonian aesthetic frequently isolates the initiate from the "funkified down low." These factors, coupled with a mutual and irrational contempt by each god for its counterpart, make the happy marriage of Apollo and Dionysius an infrequent accident.

Playwright, saxophonist, and heavy drinker Howard Moore once recounted the horror of his stint with the James Brown band. Often, an entire song would vamp on a single chord. It is as if we are sitting in a Yoruba village and every instrument is a drum. It is the quintessence of Nommo; the quality that imbues an inanimate object with ritual meaning. Soul, groove, funk, swing, in the pocket, "there," all are Americanizations of the mystic process whereby West African artisans imbue a formerly lifeless totem with spirit.

It ain't the lyric that puts ants in your pants. The three note melodies that Howard Moore played between naps on the bandstand weren't letters home to Lucy. I love the Godfather of Soul but it sho' ain't his juke joint voice that thrills the children. Still, when he squealed, "Get up'a!!!" everybody with two shoes and a breath mint hit the dance floor.

Often theatre will try to capture that ethereal but necessary quality through casting. The off-Broadway production of *A Nite In The Life Of Bessie Smith* employed legendary singer Odetta as the blues great. She, like Taj Mahal, Willie Dixon and the like, has devoted her life to the study of so-called "folk music." I watched her enthrall Rev. Jesse Jackson and the audience at Operation Push headquarters with only a microphone and a field holler. Pure, unadulterated Nommo; the voice of West Africa transported across the murderous Atlantic, escaping as a doleful mind-numbing work song on a plantation summer in Alabama.

Forced to recreate the experience for a Baptist shout section in the cabaret drama *All Roads Lead Home*, James McBride and I wrote a succession of failed songs. We re-lyricized, re-melodized, re-started yet could not capture that ancient quality that makes the fanning fat lady in an ugly hat get up and dance at Union Baptist Church just around the corner from Marian Anderson's house. Later in the same show, the same actress sings the title song in the same setting as her drug-addicted father disappears for the last time out the door at the back of the church. Nommo. During rehearsals for the New York production of the urban opera *Bobos*, I watched the creative team of Grammy award winning composer James McBride, Tony award winning music director Linda Twine and Count Basie orchestra pianist George Caldwell negotiate music rehearsal time. Ms Twine is one of the most meticulous vocal coaches on Broadway and demands perfect elocution. Her style appeared antithetical to the goal of groove except that this schoolmarmish genius has married style and substance in a miraculous way. In this, the fifth production of the award-winning show, the articulation of the libretto was inseparable from the meaning of the words and the tone of the moment. The contours of melody and the elements of intonation were taught as a single action. The note, the word and the moment were encoded together in the minds and throats of the seventeen performers so that the audience witnessed an invocation of the soul of this music.

Joseph Campbell spoke once of artists as Shamans and/or Hunans. One is the character from various world religions who takes messages to the Gods on behalf of suffering mortals. The other is the person in possession religions who invites the holy spirits into themselves so that mortals may have audience with the divine. Effective collaboration in musical theatre requires the creative team to perform both functions.

Years of "shedding" (practicing methodically) remove the technical impediments to the fluid movement of ideas. A slavish attention to craft is required in order to ultimately work freely. Ornette Coleman band alumnus and PEW fellowship recipient Bobby Zankel sounds like a Martian when he plays but practices scales like a conservatory auditioner. It is the chariot of Apollo that conveys him to the land of Nommo.

Melody, lyric, counterpoint, theme, harmony, etc. are always present or implied in the music, but in differing combinations of emphasis. Rico Bembry, a Seattle-based drummer turned composer, used piano as a percussion instrument and challenged me to extract melodies from a mass of polyrhythms. Collaborating in Houston, Texas, on an instrumental ballad with my brother Christopher began with a focus exclusively upon a saxophone-voiced motif (an engaging music phrase), then continued to repeated piano reharmonizations.

Tiny Black Spectrum Theatre in Queens, NY could not afford a composer of the caliber with whom I had become accustomed when they commissioned *The Strange Career of John Hopewell*, so I penned both the book and the seven song score. My analysis of Scott Joplin rags revealed the traditional and altered blues structures underlying many of the creations. The New Orleans-style funeral march follows the cycle of fifths popularized by classically trained bebop artists like Dizzy Gillespie. The pop tune was constructed chromatically in three descending whole tones (in other words, "Three Blind Mice.") The rock song "Sex, Drugs, Rock & Roll" didn't bother disguising its blues roots; it just displayed them loudly.

On and on the cultural appropriations continue. Today, Larry Graham's thumbed bass guitar screams, "Funk!"; tomorrow a violin free cadenza positions melody at the center of the landscape. It is as if there is a single music, viewed like an elephant by a company of soldiers on a moonless night. Our biases inform the interpretations of the event.

The obvious but often overlooked reality is that cultures meet like clasping hands. The exchange is inevitably mutual. The overseer hums a Yoruba work song on his way to a clog party while a weary slave mother sings a Brahms lullaby to the master's choleric child. There are elephant bones in opera and Persian rugs in an office of the Grand Old Opry.

Recognition of the complete inextricability of world music frees the creative mind from inhibiting constraints, and the appreciative ear is set loose to find the familiar in any joyous sound springing from the throat of a two-legged creature.

"It's all music."

***

BIBLIOGRAPHY

Afnan, Ruhi Muhsen. *Zoroaster's Influence*, Philosophical Library Inc., 1969.

Bernal, Martin. *Black Athena: Volume I*, Harvard University Press, 1987.

Finley, M.I. *The Ancient Greeks*, The Viking Press 1963.

Fortes, Meyers. *Oedipus And Job In West African Religion*, Cambridge University Press 1959..

Gagarin, Michael. *Aeschylean Drama*, University of California Press, 1976.

Hadas, Moses, ed. *The Complete Plays Of Sophocles*, Bantam Books 1967.

Hawkes, Jacquetta. *Man And The Sun*, Random House Press, 1962.

Kitto, H.D.F. *Sophocles: Dramatist And Philosopher*, Greenwood Press, 1958.

Kurtiz, Paul. *The Making Of Theatre History* Prentis Hall, Inc., 1988.

Long, Charlotte R. *The Twelve Gods Of Greece And Rome*, E.J. Brill Press, 1967.

Moore, John Andrew. *Sophocles and Arete*, Harvard University Press, 1938.

Munder, John, PhD. and Pollack, George H., MD, eds. *The Oedipus Papers*, International University Press Inc., 1988.

Paglia, Camile. *Sexual Personae, Sex And Decadence From Nefertiti To Emily Dickerson*, Vintage Press, 1991.

Richards, James A., ed. *The Outline Of Knowledge: Vol. Xvi,* J.A. Richards Inc., 1924.

Snowden, Frank N. *Blacks In Antiquity,* Harvard University Press 1970.

Soyinka, Wole. *Myth, Literature And The African World,* Cambridge University Press, 1976.

Traore, Bakary. *The Black African Theatre And Its Social Functions,* Ibadan University Press, 1972.

Vellacott, Philip, translator with introduction by him. *Aeschylus, PENGUIN BOOKS* 1961.

Webster, T.B.L. *Introduction To Sophocles,* Oxford Press, 1936.

Williams, David, compiler. *Peter Brook: A Theatrical Casebook,* Methuen Press, 1988.

ABOUT THE AUTHOR

Ed Shockley, MFA, is author of more than fifty plays, several screenplays, essays, and two collections of poetry. He is best known for the urban opera, *Bobos,* (co-authored with James McBride) and the 1981 Audelco Award winning work, *Bessie Smith: Empress of the Blues*, that set box office records at theatres across America. Other notable plays include *The Liars' Contest* and the stage adaptation of Mildred D. Taylor's novel, *Roll of Thunder Hear My Cry*. Other works include *The Box* and *Bedlam Moon*. He has won the Stephen Sondheim Award For Outstanding Contributions To American Musical Theatre, the Richard Rogers Award, HBO New Writers Project, the American Minority Playwright Festival Award, the Lila Wallace/Readers Digest production award, and two Pennsylvania State Arts Council Playwriting Fellowships. He was a featured artist in both the New York ASCAP and the Disney/ASCAP Music Theatre Workshops with Charles Strauss and Stephen Swartz respectively. Ed served as Artistic Director of the Philadelphia Dramatist Center for ten years, founder and Artistic Director of American Concert Theatre, and participated in the founding or renovation of numerous arts in education programs such as the Rainbow Company (American Music Theatre Festival), Philadelphia Young Playwrights Festival, Solaris Dance-Theatre And Video and the Mosaic Theatre Company. His short film, *Stone Mansion*, directed by J.J. Goldberger, has won festival awards worldwide and been broadcast on Showtime Cable Television and PBS network TV. Current projects include a new short film, *Badman*, directed by Tony Vinto; script consulting for the new Fox Pictures project, *Spirit Awakening*, and an innovative new play, *The Oracle*.

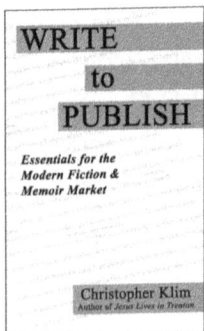

.

www.ingramcontent.com/pod-product-compliance
Lightning Source LLC
Chambersburg PA
CBHW022022090426
42739CB00006BA/240